MERIDIAN

Crossing Aesthetics

Werner Hamacher

& David E. Wellbery

Editors

Translated by
Peggy Kamuf

*Stanford
University
Press*

———

*Stanford
California
1996*

THE MUSES

Jean-Luc Nancy

Assistance for this translation
was provided by the
French Ministry of Culture

The Muses was originally published in French
in 1994 under the title *Les Muses*
© 1994 Editions Galilée

Stanford University Press
Stanford, California

Printed in the United States of America

CIP data appear at the end of the book

Stanford University Press publications are distributed
exclusively by Stanford University Press within the United
States, Canada, Mexico, and Central America; they are
distributed exclusively by Cambridge University Press
throughout the rest of the world.

Contents

Abbreviations

The following abbreviations have been used in the text for selected works by Hegel that are repeatedly cited.

A   *Aesthetics: Lectures on Fine Arts.* Trans. T. M. Knox. Oxford: The Clarendon Press, 1975.

PR   *Lectures on the Philosophy of Religion,* vol. 2. Ed. Peter C. Hodgson. Trans R. F. Brown, P. C. Hodgson, and J. M. Stewart. Berkeley: University of California Press, 1987. Unless otherwise noted, quotations are from the lectures of 1824.

PS   *The Phenomenology of Spirit.* Trans. A. V. Miller. Oxford: Oxford University Press, 1977.

THE MUSES

§ 1 Why Are There Several Arts and Not Just One?

(Conversation on the Plurality of Worlds)

The Muses get their name from a root that indicates ardor, the quick-tempered tension that leaps out in impatience, desire, or anger, the sort of tension that aches to know and to do. In a milder version, one speaks of the "movements of the spirit." (*Mens* is from the same root.) The Muse animates, stirs up, excites, arouses. She keeps watch less over the form than over the force. Or more precisely: she keeps watch forcefully over the form.

But this force springs up in the plural. It is given, from the first, in multiple forms. There are Muses and not the Muse. Their number may have varied, as well as their attributes, but the Muses will always have been several. It is this multiple origin that must interest us, and it is also the reason why the Muses, as such, are not the subject here; they are merely lending their name, this name that is multiplied from the first, so that we may give a title to this question: Why are there several arts and not just one?

~

Assuming at least, as one must, that our question itself can be maintained in its uniqueness and in its unity of question. Assuming, then, that one can arrive at the principle of a sufficient reason for thinking this plurality, and that plurality itself will not end up appearing, here, in stead and in place of principle. What might one mean by a principle (or a reason or an essence) that would not be a principle *of* plurality, but the plural itself as principle? And in what way must this properly belong to the essence of art?

~

But first of all: must the question "Why are there several arts?" be posed? Is it right to pose it?

There are two simple and well-known ways to impugn the question, to avoid it, or even, quite simply, to fail to remark it as a question.

1. First way: One is content to affirm that plurality is a given of the arts. To tell the truth, one does not even affirm it; one observes it—and who would not be forced to make this observation? That is why, most often, one does not question this plurality; one merely submits it to the test of a "classification" or (formerly) a "hierarchy" of the arts. But one is not sure how to order this classification itself, which is, moreover, why it has undergone so many variations in the course of history, not only as regards its internal distribution (how does one order the recognized arts?), but also as regards the extension of its jurisdiction (what must be recognized as an art?). One would have to undertake a classification of classifications and evaluate the specter of the diversity of the arts according to the theories of the arts. One can imagine the immensity of the task, especially if one had to extend it to the diversity of the attributes of the arts (for example: music as art of sounds, time, or space; painting as art of vision or the visible, of light or color, etc.). But the question we will call "ontological," concerning the unity of this plurality, is not posed. Either the unity is presupposed as a vague unity of subsumption—"art" in general—or else one receives the plurality without interrogating its own order, the *singular plural* of art, of the arts. This question is even, usually in a very visible manner, the question that is *skipped* by the great majority, if not by all, of these theories, whether they are crude or elaborate, empirical or transcendental. (One might add that there is nothing equivalent, in this domain, to the principle that governs, at least in a

regulative manner, the domain of the sciences—namely, mathematization. But this does not mean that the plurality of the sciences should not, as well, be examined.)

Adorno goes so far as to declare: "Most works of art fall short of coinciding with a generic concept of art. . . . Art is not a generic concept for the various types or species of art." He means to affirm, on the contrary, "the free movement of discrete moments (which is what art is all about)."[1] All the same, he does not analyze this *discreteness* in and of itself. Moreover, as one may remark, he barely evokes in proper terms the diversity of the "kinds" of art, which he tends to let be covered over by the multiplicity of "works" and which he therefore does not submit as such to the regime of the question. He is nevertheless certainly one of those who comes closest to that gesture, for he also writes: "the arts do not vanish completely in art."[2]

Setting aside Adorno, then, one may suspect, in a general manner, that if the ontological question of the *singular plural* of the Muses is dodged, this is because it is understood *a priori* that we are in the register not of ontology, but of technology. Whether technology can make an ontology, or can imply it—that question is not posed.

2. Second way: One may also rely on the affirmation that there is one art, an essence of art. This is ordinarily the "philosophical" response (which does not mean that it is only present in putatively "philosophical" texts; it can be found in many declarations by artists). Are there really several arts? Is what we apprehend as a plurality not in the final analysis the set of manifestations or the moments of a unique reality (of a unique Idea, substance, or subject), or does it not form the expressive profusion of a unique gesture, of a selfsame essential drive?

At this extremity of the specter, it can even happen that "art" oversteps its own distinction (or discreteness). Thus Heidegger can declare, in the 1956 Addendum to *The Origin of the Work of Art*, that in this essay "art is considered neither an area of cultural achievement nor an appearance of spirit; it belongs to the *disclosure of appropriation* by way of which the 'meaning of Being' can alone be defined."[3] Not only does art not reside essentially in the diversity either of its "modalities" or its "works," it does not even reside any longer in art. Its singularity is still just around the bend, all the more dignified by being less perceptible as "art" and even less as the multiplicity of artistic practices.

∼

In one way or another, art would thus be in default or in excess of its own concept. One could also say: "art" never appears except in a tension between two concepts of art, one technical and the other sublime—and this tension itself remains in general without concept.

This does not mean that it is necessary, nor, if it is necessary, that it is possible to subsume it in a concept. But it does mean that we cannot avoid thinking this tension itself. Art and the arts interbelong to each other [*s'entr'appartiennent*] in a tense, extended mode in exteriority, without any resolution in interiority. Would art then be *res extensa, partes extra partes*?

∼

It will not be pointless to recall what everyone knows: how the West came to speak of "art" and the "arts" after having spoken of the Muses.

We have been saying "art" in the singular and without any other specification only recently, only since the romantic period. (One must add that in French we said "art" under the influence of the German *Kunst*, which was already specified in this sense.) Earlier, at the time of Kant and Diderot, people said the "beaux-arts" or "fine arts," and these were often distinguished further from "belles-lettres." (At the same time, there was already a dominant tendency to place the order and essence of all these practices under "poetry"; we will return to this.) Still earlier, the *arts*, either mechanical or liberal (yet another diversity), had little to do with our *art*. (At most, one can locate a distinction of the arts of *imitation*, according to a tradition that goes back to Aristotle and Plato, but it does not clearly align with the division between the mechanical and the liberal.)

To conclude, and as we know, this linguistic anamnesis takes us from "art" to "technics."[4] What had already singularized itself in the name of the Muses as *pars pro toto* (but was there properly speaking a *totum* of the chorus of the Muses? that is the whole question)—in other words, music—was the *tekhnē mousikē*. And as we also know, what we moderns mean by "art" seems to have little to do with technics. (The recognition or the search for a "technological aesthetic," in whatever form, changes nothing, but rather confirms the gap that one would like to straddle or reduce.) Art and technics are so distinct for us that the title "art and technics," which has been the theme of more than one essay and more than one exhibition, is necessarily understood as the assertion of a problem and not as a tautology. A careful examination would, no doubt, show that a formula of the type "art and/or technics" could in its own way condense the enigma of our time, of a time that would come to recognize itself as equipped, even to excess, with a thinking about art without an invention of art, and with a profusion of technique without any thinking of technics. But the two, let us note, are united in opposition, by their common opposition to what we still sometimes call "nature." Such are, at least, the appearances, our appearances.

But no doubt there are other things to think, and our question, taken against this background of linguistic anamnesis, might also mean: Why are there now two senses of the word "art"? Why are there art and technics, in such a way that one is not the other, and that in many ways they exclude each other, and the path from one to the other is anything but guaranteed?

Why did art divide itself? And why did it divide itself in such a way that on one side, the side of "art," the unity of the presumed genus seems at least indifferent to and at most rebellious against the plurality of the presumed species, while on the other side, that of "technics," the unity of the genus—and we need not demonstrate this—is immediately understood as effectuated in a plurality of species that are multiplied indefinitely?

~

Did this division happen to art during our history, or is it not, rather, congenital to art? Has art ever had the unity that we project onto the use of a word?

In Plato an internal division is already indicated within the entire order of the *poiēseis ergasiai tekhnais*, creations produced by techniques or by arts:[5] *pars pro toto*, the part of the *tekhnai* that includes music and metrics is given the name *poiēsis*. This first, immemorial division, delivered up like a raw fact of language, separates in effect the various techniques from themselves and sets aside, along with *poiēsis*, what will become, no doubt not by accident, the name of the major pretender to first place among the beaux-arts, or even to the role of index of their essence. (*"All art . . .* is, as such, *poetry* [Dichtung]," declares Heidegger, who admittedly distinguishes *Dichtung* from *Poesy*, "the linguistic work, the poem in the narrower sense," but only in order to add right away that the latter "has a privileged position in the domain of the arts."[6] "Poetry and/or technics": doubtless, in many regards this is the Heideggerian formulation of the modern problem. And doubtless, as well, the plurality of the arts vanishes there, as does that of techniques.)

The division separates, then, the name of the product, *poiēsis*, from the name of the process or the mode of production, *tekhnē*. What has thus divided at the origin is the producing action, *ergasia* or *ergazomai*, the act whose subject is *dēmiourgos*, the one who works, who puts to work. The work has been divided, not according to the multiplicity of the ways in which it is put to work, but according to two poles, each of which tends toward unity: the product and the production, or, in other terms, the finite operation and the infinite operation. Between the two, uninterrogated, is the diversity of the works and of the modes of work.

Between the two, as well, is a way in which each of the two poles wants to know nothing about the other, which is why it is not surprising that there should arise, finally, the extreme tension between art and technics—a tension whose *pathos* itself oscillates between repulsion and attraction.

One would have to run through all the moments of history that end up there: how the sets "arts" and "techniques" are successively determined; what practices pass from one to the other and for what reasons; how the new division comes about between the Greek and Latin names for production, between the artificial and the artistic, between engineering and genius; which arts are reputed to be "beautiful" and why techniques get installed initially under the sign of a hitherto unknown ugliness; why, finally, this tension gets exacerbated and confused at the same time, the beaux-arts exhibiting their processes and materials of production while technical practices take on the aura of "design"—and how this signal jamming, this uneasiness makes possible and necessary the question we are trying to pose.

∼

Here we will examine only how the modern regime of *art* gets established in the singular, in a singular that is tendentiously nonplural (which goes against the primary meaning of *singuli*, "one by one"). We will do so in a schematic fashion, since these episodes are well known. This establishment is philosophical—as is all of its history since Plato. We are quite aware that the temper of the times is to reproach philosophy for its exploitation or its interpretation of art. But "art" itself, its face-to-face with "technics," and the doubtful, poorly examined status of the plurality of the arts are philosophical determinations. What we need to bring into question is an aspect of what the philosophical gesture will have made manifest *and* of what it will have left in the shadows. The question of the plurality of the arts, against the background of the question "art and technics"—that *is* the question of the uses and abuses of philosophy as regards *demiurgy* in general, or of the limits it sets for itself by the very construction of its concepts of art and of technics. (Adorno calls this: "Art and the misery of philosophy.")[7]

A scenario can be presented in three acts: Kant, Schelling, Hegel.

For Kant, the division of the beaux-arts goes without saying. Their diversity is a given; it is just a matter of dividing it up. This is done by "analogy of art with the mode of expression of which men avail themselves in speech," namely, the tripartition "*word, deportment*, and *tone*" ("arts of *speech*, the *figurative* arts, and the art of the *play of sensations*").[8] All the same, this partition contains the seed of its own reduction, for Kant declares: "It is only by the combination of these three kinds of expression that communication can be complete," without asking himself about the privilege that thereby remains conferred upon language. In all good logic, Kant should then be surprised by the absence of a unique art, one which would correspond to perfect communication. Lacking such a perfect art, which is not even evoked, we can at least encounter a "combination of beautiful arts in one and the same product,"[9] and it is three species of such a combination (*tragedy in verse, didactic poem, oratorio*) that turn out to fit the "presentation of the sublime, so far as it belongs to beautiful art." Everything thus gets out played out again one more time: the privilege of language, a tripartition without explication (why are there several arts for just one sublime?), and finally a "presentation" that takes charge of something that by rights goes beyond the proper domain of the arts and that no doubt forms the seed of "Art" in the absolute sense. Something of the "sublime" escapes from the plurality of the arts, disdains it or dissolves it, even goes beyond art.

Second act, Schelling: Not more than twelve years after the third *Critique*, Schelling explains in his course on the philosophy of art that art effects the "representation of the absolute with absolute indifference of the universal and the particular *within the particular*," which defines the symbol and whose supreme form is language.[10] Thus the difference between the domains of art can be explained, for example, as follows: "The formative arts are only the dead word, and yet nonetheless *word*, the act of speaking. . . . In contrast, on the lower level, in music, that living element that has passed over into death—the word *spoken* into the finite—is still perceptible only as sonority."[11] Art has found or produced its unity.

Not only does the diversity of the arts no longer go without saying, but it is in principle (in the strongest sense of the expression) subsumed into an essential—and infinite—unity.

Third act, Hegel: This time, the "inherently solid unity" of art and the differentiation of its historical "forms" demand once again, as their third dialectical moment, "the purely *external* reality" which must be that of the "*particular arts.*"[12] In this respect, "the Ideal is now resolved into its factors or moments and gives them an independent subsistence . . . because it is precisely the art-forms themselves which acquire their determinate existence through the particular arts." This independence is indeed, in one sense, absolute, for it corresponds to the fundamental law of art, which is the manifestation of the Idea as such in exteriority as such. Thus, although Hegel feels obliged to add that this independence does not prevent the possibility that the arts "may interfere with one another, may have an essential relation to one another, and supplement each other"—which supposes that the independence of the arts still leaves pending the completion of art—the moment of separate exteriority is nevertheless essential to the very essence of art.

In a certain way, the modern tension is at its height from the outset. The plurality of the arts is as essentially irreducible as the unity of art is absolute. What makes this tension possible—and which could be shown to affect the whole of Hegel's *Aesthetics*—is without a doubt the fact that art is supposed to dissolve and sublate its own end in the element of thought. How this supreme operation gets blocked and fails to reach its end, we will not show here.[13] We will retain merely that the self-overcoming of art has as its absolute corollary and symmetry what one might call the induration of the arts in an irreducible material difference.

~

This difference seems to propose itself right away as the difference between the senses. Nothing, it seems, any longer makes sense other than this: the difference between the arts has to do with the difference between the senses. And such is indeed Hegel's proposition: "art too is there for apprehension by the senses, so that, in

consequence, the specific characterization of the senses and of their
corresponding material . . . must provide the grounds for the division of the individual arts."[14]

At this point, the question of the difference between the arts
ought to be transformed into the question of the difference between the senses. Perhaps in fact they are the same question. But
how is one to understand this identity?

The most common implicit version—the one that we all more or
less consciously carry around with us—comes down to saying that
the division between the senses, which is itself taken for granted,
constrains, carves up, and limits artistic expression. In that case, art
remains by rights unique and beyond the senses, even if this status
is still vague. If, on the contrary, art is in fact conceived as having to
be "for the senses," that is, if the moment or the meaning of its
truth and its activity is in the senses, one nonetheless implies that it
is not there just to supply additional sensory stimulations. (Let it be
said in passing that the whole question of art could be posed thus:
why these sensations that are supposedly *supplementary*? In addi-
tion to what and in the place of what?)

The relation between the two differences, therefore, that between the arts and that between the senses, does not let itself be
treated lightly. Their identity and their difference contain no less
than the structure and the stakes of the *sense* and/or the *senses* of
what is called, perhaps too quickly, "art."

It is all the more difficult to treat lightly the relation between
these two differences, or these two spacings, because one is quickly
led to another sort of consideration: the difference between the
senses—that is, the five senses and the supplementary difference or
differences that are always introduced there by a desire to group
and/or to hierarchize—this difference, which is itself plural and for
a long time now registered as a *topos* (see n. 14 to this chapter), is
perhaps, in the final analysis, but the result of an "artistic" operation, or the artifact produced by a "technical" perspectivizing of
perception. In a word, the distribution or distributions of the
senses, rather than sensibility as such, would themselves be the
products of "art." We will not undertake the analysis of this pro-

duction. Perhaps it cannot be brought to term (i.e. completed, concluded) if a unique principle of "art" cannot be found outside of an intrinsic diversity, of which "sense" would itself be a name or an index. In other words, we would be spinning in a circle. But perhaps it is indeed a matter of a circle, of what it will perhaps be necessary to consider, in a mode analogous to that of the "hermeneutic circle," as an *aisthetic circle*.

～

Without being able to linger over a close examination of the difficulties encountered by all attempts at a simple derivation of the arts from the senses and/or in view of the senses, let us briefly gather together their determinant reasons.

1. The heterogeneity of the senses is not homothetic to that of the arts. (Hegel himself points this out right away; if the observation does not create any real difficulty for him, it is because he holds in reserve, on the one hand, a systematic deduction of the rationality of the five senses, thus their homogenization, and, on the other, a self-overcoming of the sensibility of art. We will not linger over this.) The classical distribution of the five senses either does not refer to five arts or raises infinite problems of the "minor" arts (e.g., cooking, perfumery). As for touch, which is established by a very long tradition as the paradigm or even as the essence of the senses in general, it does not open onto any kind of art. (When it is said that sculpture is an art of touch, one means touch at a distance— which may well be also the essence of touch, but that does not do away with what, in sculpture, exceeds touch.) Yet one may remark that art in general cannot not *touch*, in all the senses of the word (and it is even this purpose, this "for the senses" as Hegel would have it, that sets aside any moral or intellectual purpose; it is what requires that, in a certain sense at least, there is only "art for art's sake").

2. The heterogeneity of the senses is itself impossible to decide: one may, for example, consider the role of what Aristotle calls

"common-objects" (movement, figure, size), or one may look at pain as a specific sense,[15] or yet again one may take account of contemporary physiology and considerably exceed the five senses so as to envision, beyond the common-objects of Aristotle, the senses of acceleration or the tension of organs; what is more, one can attempt to take in the whole of the animal kingdom and envision distributions via "mechanoreceptors" (pressure, contact, vibration, stretching, etc.), "thermoreceptors," "photoreceptors," "chemoreceptors," "electroreceptors," or yet again, according to different criteria, via "exteroreceptors," "proprioreceptors" (actions of the body on itself), "interoreceptors" (digestion, arterial pressure, urogenital sensations, etc.).

3. Physiologists concede that any partition remains unsatisfactory and requires that one appeal to a notion of "sensorial integration." Thus there always comes a moment when sensuous unity must be reestablished over and against sensorial abstraction. What might seem to be a response to this appeal is synesthetic unity or "correspondences" (Baudelaire, Verlaine, Debussy, among others), which come to be claimed in an obvious historical correlation with the position of "art" in the singular and of the reference to "genius," as well as with the postulation of "total art." But one quickly realizes that perceptive integration and its lived experience would be more correctly located at the opposite extreme from artistic experience and that poetic "correspondences" do not belong to the register of perceptive unity, which has no knowledge of "correspondence" as such and knows only integrated simultaneity (integrated, moreover, according to a strict process of selection or abstraction: we are told that the brain puts to work only 1 percent of the approximately twenty megabits of sensory information it receives every second; whatever meaning such a measurement may have, one can say that perception is precisely not made "for the senses").[16]

In fact, when one relates the arts to the senses, one is most often obeying in an obscure fashion a double logic (which could be illustrated in an exemplary manner by Hegel):

(a) the logic of exteriority, of "sensuous presentation," or of the externalization of the Idea that is supposed to constitute the Truth of art;

(b) the logic of a homology with the living, sensuous unity (with sensibility as proper attribute of life), which turns out in the final analysis to be a logic of imitation and which comes up against, at one extreme, all the known difficulties of the theories of imitation, and, at the other extreme, all the known aporias of the claims to "total art" (aporias which Kant probably foresaw when he hesitated about the art of the sublime). What is more, the two orders of difficulty refer back one to the other: art is not imitative and life does not furnish its model.

To get beyond this antinomy, one can only envision a different synesthesia in nature, *another* sensuous integration, a proper sense of art (or of the senses in art). It is this "sense" that will be born (or at least baptized) with the aesthetics of the eighteenth century and that romanticism will have inherited. The anonymous author of the poem "Des Sens," published in 1766, thus writes:

> Ce goût du Beau, ce sens métaphysique,
> Est un sixième sens, dont l'ineffable prix,
>   Pour tant de vulgaires esprits
> N'est qu'un être problématique
>
> This taste for Beauty, this metaphysical sense,
> Is a sixth sense, whose ineffable prize
>   For so many vulgar minds
> Is but a problematical being.[17]

But a sixth sense, in the sense not only of an additional sense but of a sense that surpasses the senses (*super*sensuous), such a sense is necessarily a sense of the assumption of the senses—that is, of their dissolution or of their sublimation.

Unless it is a matter of thinking a *meta*physical sense of the "physical" that remains "physical," therefore sensuous and singularly plural. This is doubtless the core of the problem. The *singular plural / singular*[18] is the law and the problem of "art," as it is of "sense" or of the sense of the senses, of the sensed sense of their sensuous difference. A comparison could be made here to the immateriality of the soul as proved by the neo-Platonic tradition: the soul *feels* because it is wholly in every feeling part of the body, and yet it is not in any part and it is not any body. The same reasoning works for each isolated sense: a sense as such is indivisible from its *sensing*. That is why "the more a sense is reduced, the more it is penetrating": so it can be said of the vision that occurs through the pupil of the eye and of the vision of self by the soul, which occurs without any localizable extension.[19] But one is then reasoning as if nonspace could be the extreme reduction of space, or else, in the opposite case, as if the reduction supposed the extension that it reduces . . .

4. If, by contrast, one stuck to the heterogeneity of the senses, there are two paths one might follow:
—either, with Aristotle, one could consider in each sense the double movement of undergoing[20] and putting-to-work, the second belonging to the order of the *logos*, but of a *logos* which itself, according to a singular plural, is but the "feeling itself"[21] of "feeling" or its "pronouncing itself" on feeling as such, in its singularity;[22]
—or else one remains at the material and "pathic" pole of the senses, at their simple heterogeneity, and one carries forward the question of its principle: in Plato or in Aristotle, one encounters the heterogeneity of the *elements*; following the example of a modern physiology, one would add to the differentiation of material states or of bodies the differentiation of a state defined by "irritability," itself in turn differentially attuned to different states of the milieu. One will then, as we may see, have produced merely what might be called a "hyletic circle," meaning the circle of the self-relation of the material differentiation as such, or of matter as differentiation itself and, consequently, as the relation itself. This circle—from differentiated matters to materiality as difference—would be nothing other than that of a heterogeneity of the origin and of an origin of heterogeneity. Therefore, one must say either

that the heterogeneity of the arts derives from it—but one will not be able to explain in this fashion its properness in relation to material and sensual heterogeneity in general, of which it would be simply a specification—or else that the arts and "art" are properly the mode of constitution or presentation (more exactly, of constitutive presentation) of this originary circle. (That, let us note in passing, would not exclude, either by right or in the long term, the arts or techniques that are called sciences. But this is another question.)

~

Thus neither the senses as such nor their integration are either conditions or models of the arts. Instead, what goes on is similar to Freud's analysis of preliminary pleasure—an analysis which, we should recall, Freud relates, through a chiasmus or a parallel, to the analysis of the other *Vorlust* he identifies in the aesthetic "incentive bonus."[23] The *Vorlust* has two connected characteristics: that of tension and incompletion, on the one hand, and that of "zonal" diversity, on the other. And just as in the sexual order the final "discharge" annuls erotic excitation, so in the aesthetic order the satisfaction granted to the drives is no longer of an aesthetic sort. Moreover, Freud uses the same word, *Reiz*, to designate arousal and charm. Erotic and aesthetic sensualities take place right at a diversity that sets itself apart from integration or unity.

(One could add here a remark that would situate exactly the chiasmus of the two registers: to the extent that this diversity is the same, since it is that of the order of the sensuous or the "form," one cannot subordinate the aesthetic to the erotic or the erotic to the aesthetic. But their reciprocal heterogeneity would form a chiasmus by means of which there occurs a singular relation to itself *of* heterogeneity in general. The eroticism in art or of art, on the one hand, and the arts or techniques of love, on the other hand, cannot be thought in another context. This context also includes, no doubt, the parallel that Plato puts into play between the use of the word *poiēsis* for a single kind of technical production, and the use of the word *eros* for a single kind of love. If *eros* is thought as *poiēsis*—namely, as *poiēsis* "of beauty," and of a beauty that goes in a continuous line from "bodies" to "science"—*poiēsis* could well be thought of as *eros*. Freud would then be, in his way and along with several others, the inheritor of this chiasmus or this interlacing.) The erotogenic zones have no value in themselves; they are not defined by a purpose. Freud writes: "It seems probable that any part of the skin and any sense-organ—probably, indeed, any organ—can function as an erotogenic zone."[24] As for the erotogenic function, it is defined only by the increase of arousal in view of discharge: "The part played by the erotogenic zones, however, is clear. What is true of one of them is true of all. They are all used to provide a certain amount of pleasure by being stimulated in the way appropriate to them. This pleasure then leads to an increase in tension which in its turn is responsible for producing the necessary motor energy for the conclusion of the sexual act."[25] Against a background of qualitative indifference, then, the zones have, in a paradoxical manner, a quantitative function. What has to be understood is that their character as zones, their discreteness (in the mathematical sense), and their heterogeneity come from this function: in saying quantity, one also says additive growth and discontinuity. And in saying desire, one also says "greater pleasure of satisfaction." Desire (the tension of the *Vorlust*) *is the discreteness of pleasure.*

Whatever one might otherwise say about the energetic model, it at least has the function here of granting a discontinuity and a dislocation of pleasure, or of the *aisthēsis* in general,[26] which would mean, by the same token, of the *aisthēsis* insofar as it is without any generality, or rather, insofar as it has only a dis-located generality, *partes extra partes,* not only *res extensa* in the Cartesian manner, but a general and generic being-outside-itself, a *zoned* being of the so-called "sensuous" condition.[27]

~

The qualitative indifference of the zones is exposed by the primacy of touch: it is the endpoint of the process of stimulation (immediately after visual stimulation, Freud places that of touching, whereas he declared earlier that the former derives from the latter "ultimately,"[28] as do no doubt all the others). Now, for all of tradition, touch, as we have already intimated, is nothing other than "the sense of the body in its entirety," as Lucretius puts it.[29] Touch is nothing other than the touch or stroke of sense altogether and of all the senses.[30] It is their sensuality as such, felt and feeling. But touch itself—inasmuch as it is a sense and consequently inasmuch as it feels itself feeling, or more than that, inasmuch as it *feels itself feeling itself*, since it only touches by touching also itself, touched by what it touches *and* because it touches—touch presents the proper moment of sensuous exteriority; it presents it *as such and as sensuous*. What makes for touch is "this interruption, which constitutes the touch of the *self-touching*, touch *as self-touching*."[31] Touch *is* the interval and the heterogeneity of touch. Touch is proximate distance. It makes one sense what makes one sense (what it *is* to sense): the proximity of the distant, the approximation of the intimate.

Le toucher—perhaps it would be better to say *la touche*, or else one would have to preserve the verbal value of the word, as when one speaks of "le sentir," "sensing"—thus has no "primacy" or "privilege" except insofar as it subordinates nothing to it: it is or it gives but the general extension and particular extraposition of sensing. Touch *forms one body* with sensing, or it makes of the sensing faculties a body—it is but the *corpus* of the senses.

Sensing and the sensing-oneself-sense that *makes* for sensing itself consist always in sensing at the same time that there is some other (which one senses) and that there are other zones of sensing, overlooked by the zone that is sensing at this moment, or else on which this zone touches on all sides but only at the limit where it ceases being the zone that it is. Each sensing touches on the rest of sensing as that which it cannot sense. Sight does not see sound and does not hear it, even though it is also in itself, or *right at* itself, that it touches on this nonseeing and is touched by it . . .

Indifference *or* synesthetic synergy consists in nothing other than the auto-heterology of touch. The touch or stroke of the sense may thus be distributed and classified in as many ways as one likes: what makes it into the touch that it is is a dis-location, a heterogenization in principle.

~

But what does art do if not finally touch upon and touch by means of the principal heterogeneity of "sensing"? In this heterogeneity in principle that resolves itself into a heterogeneity *of the* principle, art touches on the sense of touch itself: in other words, it touches at once on the "self-touching" inherent in touch and on the "interruption" that is no less inherent in it. In another lexicon, one might say: it touches on the immanence and the transcendence of touch. Or in still other terms: it touches on the transimmanence of being-in-the-world. Art does not deal with the "world" understood as simple exteriority, milieu, or nature. It deals with being-in-the-world in its very springing forth.

By the same token, it touches on the living integration of the sensuous—but this time, one must understand "to touch on" in the sense of shaking up, disturbing, destabilizing, or deconstructing. Art touches in this manner on that which, of itself, *phusei*, naturally, establishes the synthetic unity and the continuity of a world of life and activity. In the final analysis, that world is less a sensuous world than an intelligible world of markers, functions or uses, and transitivities—in the final analysis less a world, perhaps, than a milieu, an *Umwelt* (that of the "1 percent of information"). Art isolates or forces there the moment of the *world* as such, the being-world of the world, not as does a milieu in which a subject moves, but as exteriority and exposition of a being-in-the-world, exteriority and exposition that are formally grasped, isolated, and presented as such.

Therefore the world is dis-located into plural worlds, or more precisely, into the irreducible plurality *of* the unity "world": this is the *a priori* and the transcendental of art. It makes appear that the appearance of a world is always first of all that of phenomena, each of which is "phenomenon-of-world."[32] It brings out that a sense-of-world, and consequently the sense of the world, is only given by dis-locating at the origin its unique and unitary sense of "sense" in the general *zoning* that is sought in each of the many differential distributions of the senses.

But what art makes visible—that is, what it touches upon and what it *at the same time* puts to work through *tekhnē*—is that it is precisely not a matter of a differentiation happening to an organic unity, nor of a differential as continuous variation. It is rather a matter of this: that the unity and uniqueness of a world *are*, and are nothing but, the singular difference of a *touch* and of a *zone* of touch. There would be no world if there were no discreteness of zones (an extension more ancient than any origin): in fact, only this discreteness allows the thing to be what it is, that is, thing in itself, which does not mean "thing grasped in an essence that has re-treated to the farthest point, behind appearance," but *thing itself*, that is, still *right at* itself or *next to itself*. For a thing to have, potentially, "something" like an "interiority" or an "intimacy," it must still first be itself, and thus laid out [*disposée*] right at itself, very precisely. (One could say: superimposed on itself, and thus touching itself, near/far, *distanced in itself*.)[33]

This disposition implies a dis-position; it implicates itself as dis-position, discreteness, plurality, and heterogeneity of "zones." The latter are not at all merely diverse localizations in a homogeneous space. They are at the same time, by virtue of a spacing that is not first of all spatial but ontological ("space" is here the name of "Being"), the absolute difference of appearance or of being-in-the-world as such. This is why Heidegger could write: "We should learn to recognize that things themselves are the places, and do not merely belong in a place."[34]

Being-in-the-world (which is the being *of the* world) takes place and can take place neither according to generality (which is itself a particular *topos*, e.g., that of a discourse on art in general) nor according to universality understood as the resource of a unique-ness and a unity of origin. More exactly, the "point of view" of an *intuitus originarius* is not that of a being-in-the-world, which is why, moreover, it is not a "view." If there is a "point" (without dimension, therefore), it is that of a "creation" of the world. The creation of the world is not in the world.[35] But if creation took place, there would be for the creator, as such, no spacing, no "zoning": neither places, nor colors, nor sounds, nor smells. One would have to say instead that creation (and consequently the creator, who is nothing other than his/her act) is itself spacing and the difference between zones. This would lead one to say that creation is (the sense of) touch or the stroke of being-in-the-world.

Thus, to maintain for a moment the Kantian analogy, the *intuitus derivativus* is granted according to the touch of exteriority and the disparity of touches. But, contrary now to Kant, it is not satisfied with the forms of space and time: it must also have the multiplicity of "sensuous qualities" that make up the "in-itself" or the "right-at-itself" of the thing. Here the empirical is the transcendental. But this "empirical" is nothing that one can simply fix under categories such as "color," "sound," and so forth. There is not color "in general," there is not even red "in general." As Wittgenstein says: "To be able generally to name a colour, is not the same as being able to copy it exactly. I can perhaps say 'There I see a reddish place' and yet I can't mix a colour that I recognize as being exactly the same. . . . Imagine someone pointing to a spot in the iris in a face by Rembrandt and saying 'the wall in my room should be painted this colour.' "[36] The empirical is not a presumed "sensuous given"; it is not a *subject presumed sensuous*. The empirical is the technics of the local, the presentation of place.

~

The example of Wittgenstein is not chosen at random: it is art, and precisely art in the detail of its technique (but "detail of technique" is a pleonasm) or art as technique of the detail, that is, of difference and discreteness, that makes visible *local* color or that makes visible the fact that color *is* only *local*. Furthermore, it is here the color of a place at the center of an eye: art-technique looks, it has regard for our look [*regard*], it looks at it and causes it to come about as look. Hegel, for his part, said: "it is to be asserted of art that it has to convert every shape in all points of its visible surface into an eye . . . art makes every one of its productions into a thousand-eyed Argus, whereby the inner soul and spirit is seen at every point."[37]

This look looks by way of all the kinds and all the forms of phenomenality. Moreover, in each kind or form it multiplies itself into an infinity of points, in an infinitely divisible *locality*, even though its "points" are not geometric and without dimension, but affect each time again a determined extension. Furthermore, in each local value it combines heterogeneous sensuous values without homogenizing them: *this* red is also a thickness, a fluidity, a figure, a movement, a flash of sound, a taste, or an odor. The zone is itself zoned.

We will try, then, to distribute as follows the operation of the plurality of the arts.

1. This plurality breaks down the living unity of perception or action, but it does so in a way opposite to the abstract breakdown into sensations. (The latter is never anything more than a convenient stopgap in the service of everyday communication, and it remains at a distance from the double technical breakdown into the sciences, on the one hand, and the arts, on the other, each of them perhaps touching the other more than it appears.) It isolates what we call a "sense," or a part or feature of this sense; it isolates it so as to force it to be only what it is outside of signifying and useful perception. Art forces a sense to touch itself, to be this sense that it is. But in this way, it does not become simply what we call "a sense," for example, sight or hearing: by leaving behind the integration of the "lived," it also becomes something else, another instance of unity, which exposes another world, not a "visual" or "sonorous" world but a "pictorial" or "musical" one. It makes of the "sonorous" or "auditory" region, for example, a world composed of equivalents, pitches, scales, harmonic relations, melodic sequences, tonalities, rhythms, timbres, and so forth—a world one of whose faces, the written and calculated one, has nothing to do with sound and another of whose faces is taken up in the always unpredictable quality of a singular "interpretation" or "execution."

The world that we would be tempted to designate as the world of a sense is not a limitation of the world of synesthesia. It is another world [*monde*] or another monad. This is the force of the Muses: it is at once a force of separation, isolation, intensification, and metamorphosis. Out of something that was part of a unity of signification and representation, it makes something else, which is not a detached part but the touch of another unity—which is no longer the unity of signification. It is a suspension of the latter; it touches on meaning's extremities.

Valéry puts it this way: "The precision of things required by drawing requires in turn the collaboration of devices that, *once they have signified*, ask only to be dis-tracted. The eye leaves the object once it is named and judged as quickly as a fly that has landed and eaten on a corner of wall. After having traced a gesture, the hand tends to return by a shorter path, caught up again by the spring. . . . To make the hand free *in the sense of the eye*, one must take away its freedom *in the sense of the muscles*."[38]

Art disengages the senses from signification, or rather, it disengages the world from signification, and that is what we call "the senses" when we give to the (sensible, sensuous) senses the sense of being external to signification. But it is what one might just as correctly name the "sense of the world." The sense of the world as suspension of signification—but we now understand that such a "suspension" is touch itself. Here, being-in-the-world touches on its sense, is touched by it, touches itself as sense.

2. While so doing, art dis-locates "common sense" or ordinary synesthesia, or it causes it to touch itself in an infinity of points or zones. Difference proliferates, not only among the major sensorial registers, but across each of them: color, nuance, paste, brilliance, shadow, surface, mass, perspective, contour, gesture, movement, shock, grain, timbre, rhythm, flavor, odor, dispersion, resonance, trait, duction, diction, articulation, play, cut, length, depth, instant, duration, speed, hardness, thickness, vapor, vibration, cast, emanation, penetration, grazing touch, tension, theme and variation, *et cetera*, that is, multiplied touches *ad infinitum*. All have their Muses, or else all are Muses. Here as elsewhere, force is a

difference and a play of forces. The *vis poetica* or the *furor* of the "poet," the "magnetic" force of the Muse in Plato's *Ion*, is the force of a "divine lot."[39]

3. But while so doing, the dis-located synesthesia, properly and technically *analyzed*, sets off as well, not another synthesis, but a reference, or, in Baudelaire's terms, a *response* from one touch to another.[40] This response is neither a relation of external homology nor an internal osmosis, but what might be described, with the etymology of *re-spondere*, as a pledge, a promise given in response to a demand, to an appeal: the different touchings promise each other the communication of their interruptions; each brings about a touch on the difference of the other (of an other or several others, and virtually of all others, but of a totality without totalization). This "co-respondence" disengages itself from signification. One can say, along with Deleuze: "Between a color, a taste, a touch, a smell, a sound, a weight [and one is doubtless meant to understand that an "et cetera" prolongs this list of six "senses"—J.-L.N.], there would be an existential communication that constitutes the 'pathic' (nonrepresentative) moment of sensation in general. In Bacon's *Corridas*, for example, one hears the hooves of the animals [other examples follow]. . . . It is therefore the painter's task to *make one see* a kind of original unity of the senses and to cause a multi-sensible Figure to appear visually. But this operation is possible only if the sensation of any particular domain . . . is directly plugged into a vital power that exceeds all domains and traverses them. This power is Rhythm, which is more profound than vision, hearing, etc. . . . It is diastolic-systolic: the world that makes me by closing itself down on me, the self that opens itself to the world, and opens up the world."[41]

It will, however, be necessary to remark that the "original unity of the senses" which is invoked in this manner proves to be but the singular "unity" of a "between" the sensuous domains, that "existential communication" turns out to take place in the element of the outside-itself, of an ex-position of existence (an existential rather than an existentiell, to put it in Heidegger's terms, that is, an *a priori* condition that is not a condition of an object but of being-in-the-world), and that "Rhythm" has its proper moment only in the gap of the beat that makes it into rhythm. By this account, rhythm is not simply analogous to the synesthesia of ordinary perception in the form that Deleuze takes it over from Merleau-Ponty, nor is it, as Deleuze puts it in an "essentialist" formula, what "appears as music when it invests the auditory level, as painting when it invests the visual level": rhythm does not *appear*; it is the beat of appearing insofar as appearing consists simultaneously and indissociably in the movement of coming and going of forms or presence in general, and in the heterogeneity that spaces out sensitive or sensuous plurality. Moreover, this heterogeneity is itself at least double: it divides very distinct, incommunicable qualities (visual, sonorous, etc.), *and* it shares out among these qualities other qualities (or the same ones), which one might name with "metaphors" (such as the *dark*, the *brilliant*, the *thick*, the *soft*, the *strident*, etc., but also, through a generalized metaphorical circulation, *taste* or *flavor*, *odor*, *tone*, *color*, *flesh*, etc.), but which are in the final analysis meta-phors in the proper sense, effective transports or communication across the incommunicable itself, a general play of *mimēsis* and of *methexis* mixed together across all the senses and all the arts. The general rhythm of the sensuous or of sense is the movement of this *mimēsis/methexis* "among" forms or presences that do not preexist it, definitively, but that arise from it as such. It is, right at the forms or the presences, the mobility that raises them up as such—and that raises them much less in relation to a "ground" (perhaps there is no ground for all these figures, no other "ground" than their differences) than it raises some in relation to others, all of them being thus grounds or figures for one another.[42] Perhaps the "ground" is only the *mimēsis/methexis* according to which the arts or the senses of the arts endlessly meta-phorize each other. Contagion and transport of the Muses.

4. Thus, the arts are first of all *technical*. They are not technical "first of all" in the sense that they comprise an initial part, procedure, which is capped by a final part, "artistic" accomplishment.

The Muses do not happen upon a craftlike operation: they install it—just as we know, for example, that a specifically symbolic use of coloring agents belonged to the Anthropoids of the Paleolithic, along with the appropriate techniques of extraction, mixing, heating, transportation, stocking, permeating, or applying.[43] The arts are technical in a sense that means they may well be indissociable from what one could call, at least provisionally, the "essence of technics" and by virtue of which the couple "art and technics" would form, in our age, the internal rift and the problematic utterance that we began by remarking.

Technique means knowing how to go about producing what does not produce itself by itself. Technique is a—perhaps infinite—space and delay between the producer and the produced, and thus between the producer and him- or herself. It is production in an exteriority to self and in the discreteness of its operations and its objects. In this regard, the singular plural of art extends to the endless multiplying of the artist's technical decisions: "To make art is to judge art, to decide, to choose. 'To make something,' says Duchamp, 'is to choose a tube of blue, a tube of red, to put a little on one's palette, and always to choose the quality of the blue, the quality of red, and always choose the place in which one is going to put it on the canvas, it is always to choose.' "[44]

With regard to a representation of "nature," understood as a "bursting of a blossom into bloom, in itself," "technics" is doubtless flawed.[45] But this representation of "nature," or of *phusis*, is nothing other than the sublimated or compensatory representation *of self* that a technics at a loss for self has provided itself. (Why "at a loss"? We will not take this up here, but it is perhaps the whole affair of the West.) It is also, in a connected fashion, the representation by virtue of which art has regarded itself with suspicion throughout our whole tradition, with a suspicion to which neglect of the plurality of the arts or embarrassment before it testifies in particular.

With regard to a "nature," art lacks origin and end. That is why the Judeo-Christian idea of "creation" comes along to fill an abyss opened between "art" (or "technics") and "nature" by borrowing from both and also by refusing both. Not by chance has "creation" passed into the vocabulary and the representation of the art of genius. Along with this representation, one also closes art into the aporia of a divine autism. Yet art-technique exposes an exteriority of the work to its production or to its subject, just as it exposes an exteriority of its end: for its completed work is always in the incompletion of that which postpones the presentation of its end, its essence, or its subject—the technical work linking endlessly to other techniques and asking again endlessly for, as its most proper end, yet another technique, and consequently its end that appears to itself in the mode of a perpetual "means," for an endless end.

Technique is the obsolescence of the origin and the end: the exposition to a lack of ground and foundation, or that which ends up presenting itself as its only "sufficient reason," experiencing itself as radically insufficient and as a devastation of the ground, the "natural," and the origin. Technique extends a withdrawal of the "ground," and the most visible part of our history consists in this extension. Technique as such, in the common sense of the word, at the same time extends and recovers this *Grundlosigkeit* or *Abgründigkeit*. This is why there is not "technique" but "techniques" and why the plural here bears the "essence" itself. It might be that art, the arts, is nothing other than the second-degree exposition of technique itself, or perhaps the technique *of the ground* itself. How to produce the ground that does not produce itself: that would be the question of art, and that would be its plurality of origin.

(After all, the primitive meaning of the word *ars*, of this Latin word that translated *tekhnē*, is that of "articulation" [from the Greek *arthron*], and all articulation has the structure of a singular plural, of a division and a play. It is not a fracture but, in its way, the "fractal" symmetrical to it. Nor is it impossible, through the bias of *armus* (the shoulder joint), to compare art with the German *Art*, which means "mode," "species," "particular manner." Art is always a question of *manner*.)

How to produce the ground, in what manner, if the *ground* is not *one* and is not a *grounds* or a *fund* from which to draw one's resources?[46] Or else its resource is that of a heterogenesis. The ground does not produce itself and is not produced in any manner. The ground is the obviousness or manifestness of Being: existence, with which one cannot have done, at least as long as one does not manipulate it toward some end, existence as the "infinite multiplicity of the world."[47] But the multiplicity of the world does not remain even the multiplicity of *a* world: it qualifies the world as heterogeneity of worlds *in which consists the unity of the world.*

〜

In other words, the sensuous and technical plurality of the arts is bound up with intelligible sense. And it is thus that there is an art, or rather, once again, arts of intelligible sense, that is, arts of language, on which all the other arts touch according to modalities that irresistibly lead to attempts to inter-express them through the category of "poetry." With the endlessly renewed prevalence or domination of "poetry" and of a "poetry" (*Dichtung*) that is more essential than the "poem," we witness simultaneously the renewal of the arts beneath the unity of a pure production of sense *and* the sensuous dis-location of sense. It is in this manner that Hegel submits poetry to the contradictory double determination of having as its proper nature, on the one hand, the moment of the extenuation of the sensuous (it "reduces sound to a meaningless sign")[48] and, on the other hand, the moment of an "end in itself" of the "sensuous element" that is verbal sonority.[49] Hegel does not remark this contradiction; it thus remains stretched between two truths of poetry, of which one is its passage into and its surpassing as required by philosophical truth (which is why poetry is the art that initiates the dissolution of art), while the other is, by contrast, the "particularization to which poetry proceeds more than the other arts do,"[50] that is, the multiplicity and exteriority of its forms, genres, prosodic and tropological resources, to which poetry since Hegel would allow us to add an overabundant variety of formal variations and material contaminations.

In conformity with the history of the word, "poetry" names a division, a dissension of technical production, *and* the paradoxical (or unlocatable) production of this very dissension as essence, but "sensuous essence," if one may put it that way, of production. Production, in the singular and absolutely, is nothing other than the production of *sense*. But it thereby shows itself to be production, a literally untenable tension toward a before-ness (or behind-ness) of sense insofar as what "produces" it as such is the fact of its being first of all received, felt, in short, *sensed* as sense. (One could say: sense senses itself, and the truth, the *touch* or *stroke* of truth, is the interruption of the "sensing itself.") This tension is untenable, and that is why there is no poetry that does not bear upon the extremity of its own interruption and that does not have this movement for its law and its technique. Here Rimbaud is necessarily exemplary.

Poetry presents itself simultaneously as *pars pro toto* of art and as *totum pro parte* of technique. This chiasmus is that of intelligible sense (art of the word, *pars pro toto*) and of sensuous sense (*poiēsis*, production that is, if not material in the ordinary sense, at least regulated by the exteriority of its end).[51] But such a chiasmus is nothing other than the necessary double encroachment of one sense on another, which is far more radical and constitutive than one might be led to think by what seems to stem from a linguistic contingency (the double sense of "sense" that Hegel did not fail to remark). (Sensuous) sense senses only if it is oriented to an object and if it valorizes it in a meaningful, informative, or operational context; reciprocally, (intelligible) sense makes sense only if it is, as one says, "perceived" and the "intuitive or perceptive relation to *intelligible sense* has always included, in finite being in general, an irreducible receptivity."[52] (Sensuous) sense makes (intelligible) sense; it is indeed nothing but that, the intellection of its receptivity as such. (Intelligible) sense is sensed/senses itself; it is indeed nothing but that, the receptivity of its intelligibility. But receptivity consists *ea ipsa* in its singular plural.

Whence two questions that intersect each other indefinitely, or rather, that are incrusted in each other: What is the *aisthēsis* of significance, what is its receiving organ? and, What is its sensation, what *taste* does sense have and on which *tongue*?[53] Furthermore, what is the signification of the sensuous—by which path does it lead to its intelligibility? A double technical question, in which sense demands from itself its own condition of production, but in which it thus *demands itself*, tensed toward its own activity as toward the reception of its own receptivity, toward a *logos* that would be the *pathos* of *pathos*.

The permanent subsumption of the arts under "poetry," and the no less permanent and irreducible face-to-face of "poetry" and "philosophy," are effects of this demand to sense sense sensing (itself). Thus, the poetic subsumption is not in vain, and it indicates clearly the unique and unitary place of "art." But it does not fill this place with a substance or a subject (that is, with an infinite relation to self, with an absolute sensing-itself) except insofar as it interprets "art" in the philosophical mode, that is, as a reunion *without exteriority* of the intelligible and the sensuous. In other words: as a touching-itself that would reabsorb into itself the moment of interruption. But this requirement is contradictory if the relation to self of sense implicates itself as exteriority. Thus Hegel himself declares: "Thinking is only a reconciliation between reality and truth within thinking itself. But poetic creation and formation is a reconciliation in the form of a *real* phenomenon itself."[54] To which one must add that the "poetic" reconciliation thus takes place, but it takes place in an irreconcilable mode, according to exteriority and to an exteriority that is doubly qualified, since it is at once the exteriority of the phenomenon as such or of the sensuous as being-outside-itself, *and* the exteriority of the poetic reconciliation in relation to the thought reconciliation inasmuch as the latter is "only . . . within thinking," in other words, inasmuch as thinking cannot think itself (in truth, touch itself) except as "only thinking" or as *finite* thinking whose finitude separates it from the thing, from its most proper thing, *and* precisely renders thereby sensuous the stakes of thinking. For that very reason, thinking senses itself (feels its weight, its gravity) two times outside itself: once in the thing "itself" (that is, the thing that is the same as thinking *insofar* as the thing makes itself felt as "thing-outside," impenetrable, touchable as impenetrable), and a second time in poetry (as sensuous assumption of sense itself that thinking only thinks or in some way "pre-senses"—but all of Hegel's rigor is devoted precisely to preventing a romantic "presentiment" or an artistic effusion of thought from infiltrating at this point).

In their turn, then, thing and poetry, which together form the ex-position of thought, open between them an extension and a tension that are properly those of creation as *poiēsis* of the *thing*. But if this "creation" is not secretly governed by a mystical and romantic (and, in a sense, Heideggerian) model, it must then turn out to be a *technique* of the world. Now, "technique of the world" can only be understood in the plural of techniques that have neither the point of origin of a *fiat* nor the endpoint of a *sense*. As soon as "creation" is undone as sui generis concept (for it is an autodestructive concept), it opens the singular plural of art. Or else "art" is the name, no doubt still a provisional one, of its singular plural.

Two consequences follow from this.

—The first is that philosophy will never reduce the difference of art except in the mode of a reduction that is "only thought," and that, in these conditions, the "end of art" as its philosophical sublation is an end that one may call indifferently *infinite* or else always-already *finite* as end, that is, as destined to repeat itself. The end of art was always yesterday.

—The second is that what thereby resists the dialectic, what resists within the mediation of sense, is not only "poetry," but along with it, right away, an irreducible plurality of the arts. The poetic or poetizing subsumption turns out to be *in itself* heterogeneous. The place or the form in which art would come to touch on its essence can only be the *partes extra partes* of artistic worlds. Poetry names its proper outside, or the outside as the proper: the sense of sense.

That is what may be heard in these words of a poet: "Whenever we speak with things in this way we also dwell on the question of their where-from and where-to, an 'open' question 'without resolution,' a question which points towards open, empty, free spaces— we have ventured far out."[55]

Or yet again, from another poet:

> Because the only hidden meaning of things
> Is that they have no hidden meaning at all.

This is stranger than all the strangenesses,
And the dreams of all the poets,
And the thoughts of all the philosophers—
That things really are what they appear to be
And that there is nothing to understand

Yes, here's what my senses learned all by themselves:
Things have no meaning—they have existence.
Things are the only hidden meaning of things.[56]

∽

So sense is multiply unique, and uniquely multiple. That itself, however, needs to be specified. No more than there is a simple reciprocal exteriority of the senses, except by rather crude abstraction, and no more than there is, by contrast, a homology between a distribution of the arts and a distribution of the senses (or even material elements or states), can there be a simple multiplicity that would come in the place of the One.

Instead, multiplicity exposes unity in multiple ways. Not, however, as its diverse figures, which would then be but its representations and which would not allow one to grant the plurality of the arts. (In this sense, moreover, it is correct to say that art always disfigures, that it undoes the consistencies of presented presence.) Plurality exposes or expresses unity in the sense in which it puts unity outside itself at birth, in the sense, consequently, in which the One of unity is not One "once and for all," but takes place "every time for one," so to speak. Each one of the arts exposes in its way the unity of "art," which has neither place nor consistency outside this "each one"—still more, the unity of a single art is ex-posed in this sense only in its works one by one. Each work is in its fashion a synesthesia and the opening of a world. But it is this insofar as "the world" as such, in its being-world (the being of that *to* which opens a being-*to-the*-world),[57] is plurality of worlds.

Thus, the "in its fashion" of each art, of each style, and of each work, its *manner* or incommunicable technique, is not an expressive variation on the ground of an identical theme. It is the necessary rhythmic discreteness of a cut or a cutting out [*découpe*] of appearing. Not the cutting out that lifts up a figure against a ground, but the cut of a form inasmuch as a form *is a ground that withdraws*, that removes or ex-poses itself of itself, different from itself as ground. Thus Hubert Damisch can say of Dubuffet that his figures "do not let themselves be distracted from the ground, a ground that in its turn is treated as figure and whose lacunae the figures come to fill in, whose flaws they inhabit, until they are themselves no longer but flaws and lacunae."[58] A form is the force of a ground that sets apart and dislocates itself, its syncopated rhythm.

It is perhaps in this that the "form" or the *fashion* of the apparition consists: "What appears, in dreams and also in the theater, always proceeds from space as one of its metamorphoses. An apparition is, for a space, a provisional manner of appearing. It is never cleanly detached from this appearing. A figure is never entirely detached from the ground. It is always, more or less, the ground that comes forward as figure and that will soon move back away to become again simple space."[59]

(Moreover, to the plurality of figures in this sense, to the plurality, therefore, of *manners* that make up the arts and their techniques, one would have to add that of their relative or absolute "greatness," the plurality, in other words, that distinguishes the "major arts" from the "minor arts," including the uncertain usage governing the "arts" of conversation, love, dress, and so forth, as well as the distinction between more or less "great" styles, between "masterpieces" and "operettas." But, to conclude, so as not to be finished with it, what if the truth of the singular plural of art was in the fact that the arts are themselves *innumerable*, and of their forms, registers, calibers, touches, exchanges through *mimēsis* and *methexis* . . . ?)

Here is the limit of a phenomenology: the single theme of an "appearing" cannot respond to the clear-cut—and cutting—discreteness of a ground that withdraws and that retraces itself in forms. Or else it must be a matter of an appearing *of* appearing itself—but it is, precisely, no longer an appearing—of a coming into presence that is more ancient than any coming to light, of a coming *of* the world rather than a coming into the world, and of a signifying more ancient than any intentionality that donates sense.

In truth, it is a matter neither of a donation nor an intention, nor even of a signifying. The coming of the world is not even a coming. The world is simply *patent*, if one may understand by that an appearance that does not "appear," no immanence of a subject having preceded its transcendence, and no obscure ground its luminosity. It is an infinite patency, like that of Spinoza's truth, *qui se ipsam patefacit* ("that discloses itself") and *nullo egeat signo* ("needs no sign"). Truth, in fact, or sense of sense, is the patency of the world: that is, on the one hand, the appearing of the nonapparent, or the nonappearing of all "patency," and on the other hand, this, that there is only the world. But that does not amount to saying that art would take charge of the truth, or that it would make it appear and shine. It means rather that truth *would make art*, or more exactly, that it would be its own art—its own arts.

The things of art are not a matter for a phenomenology—or else, they *are* themselves phenomenology, according to an altogether other logic of this "-logy"—because they are in advance of the phenomenon itself. They are of the patency of the world. Or else, that's what the phenomenon is, but not in the sense of what appears in the light: rather than the *phanein*, it is the *phaos* itself, light, and not the light that appears (*lumen*) by clinging to surfaces, but the light that flashes (*lux*) and that causes to appear, itself nonapparent as such. *Lux* without *fiat*, having neither creator, subject, nor source, being the source but in itself refracted, in itself radiant, exploding, broken.

Husserl writes: "Absurdity first arises when one philosophizes and, in probing for ultimate information as to the meaning of the world, fails to notice that the whole being of the world consists in a certain 'meaning.'" One can only agree, if what is meant is that the world in the sense of "sense" is identical to the world as complete circumscription of finitude, which is its infinite circumscription. This may also be put in other terms: finitude is the sensing-itself of the infinite in action, its forcibly discrete touch.

But one no longer goes along with Husserl when he immediately adds: "a certain 'meaning' which presupposes absolute consciousness as the field from which the meaning is derived."[60] For the infinite sense that touches itself finite (that interrupts itself sensibly) is not "given," by anything or anyone and to anything or anyone. It is not "given"; it is merely patent *and* suspended in its very patency, patent-non-apparent. If it does precede itself infinitely, it is not as the subject of an intentionality but as the patency of this suspension and of its immediate "particularization." Thus, there are not "modes" of a unique "donation"; rather, "donation" itself, if one wishes to maintain this lexicon, is fragmented into its discrete modes. These modes are worlds.

Art exposes this. Which does not mean that art *represents* originary patency (which would once again amount to thinking art as being under philosophical surveillance). But *that there is art* and that there are *several arts*, this is what is exposed as patency. Or in other words: this is what is patent about patency. In a different lexicon, one could say: this is the presentation of presentation. Or still more exactly, perhaps: this is what renders patent the fact that there is patency, in general. This is what presents the fact that there is presentation, in general. And precisely because there is not presentation or patency "in general," there is only the plural presentation of the singular plural of presentation.

The presentation of presentation is not a representation: it does not relate presentation to a subject for which or in which it would take place. The presentation of presentation relates it to itself. Patency is related to itself—as if one were saying simply: *patet*, "it is manifest," "it is evident," not so as to initiate infinite reflexivity ("it is evident that it is evident"), but rather so as to make appear, to make heard, felt, and touched, the "subject" *it* of the obviousness. This *it* is uttered, on the one hand, as a *"there is* obviousness," putting the accent on the *there*, there is there, according to the multiplicity of places, spaces, zones, instants, and, on the other hand, as an "it is *it* that is obvious," "it" being neither a person nor a thing, nor a principle, nor a ground, but the singular plural of occurrences of existence, or presence, or passage.[61] That presentation should touch itself, which is to say as well, that it should remain suspended in its passage, in its coming and going.

One could also put it this way: art is the transcendence of immanence as such, the transcendence of an immanence that does not go outside itself in transcending, which is not ex-static but ek-sistant. A "transimmanence." Art exposes this. Once again, it does not "represent" this. Art is its ex-position. The transimmanence, or patency, of the world takes place as art, as works of art. And that is why these works themselves work a definitive torsion on the couple transcendence/immanence. Adorno writes: "The logical consistency and internal structuration [art works] display is borrowed directly from the model of spiritual mastery over reality. This aspect is transcendent because it is imported by art from outside. . . . However, these categories of monadology become entirely transformed in the process of being absorbed by art, losing much of their plausibility. Aesthetics must needs demand immersion in the individual works." And he adds right away, "It is the artwork itself that points beyond its monadic constitution," only to continue: "The only way to relate an aesthetic particular to the moment of universality is through its closure as a monad."[62]

In other words, and as we all know, as we all experience one day or another, it is not possible to touch (through the discourse of sense) on the work of art. It is only possible to bring this work into the medium of sense, first of all into the medium of an eventual "sense of art" as such (and of a "sense" of the word "art"), by interrupting the hold of the discourse (in conformity with the law of touch) through this "hermeticism" whereby the work touches only itself, or is to itself its own transimmanence. And this is not valid only for the work of an artist, for a style, for a genre, for each of the arts and for new "arts" to come: it is valid for the singular plural of the essence of the arts.

～

That presentation touches itself, which is also to say that we are touched (we also speak of being *moved* [émus], but this latter emotion is a suspension of the *émoi*, or agitation). That is what Pessoa says in his manner when he writes:

> The gods do not have a body and a soul,
> but solely a body, and are perfect.
> It is the body that takes the place of their soul.

Which is why, as he also puts it, "people say the gods never die"—
and the arts never die, just as they are born along with humans and
techniques. It is also why they are the *gods*, in the plural, which is to
say, having nothing of what we call the divine. The arts are older
than religion: this is, doubtless, an impossible thesis to prove, but it
is strictly obvious.[63] The Muses are daughters of Mnemosyne—not
in a single conception, but after nine nights spent with Zeus—and
they carry the memory of what comes before the divine order.

In a sense, there is a privilege of art here. But it is the privilege of
an index, which shows and touches, which shows by touching. It is
not the privilege of a superior revelation. The most difficult thing,
no doubt, in talking about art is to move the discourse away from a
sacred reverence or a mystical effusion. This is what we must begin
to do through an obstinate return from the discourse on "art" to the
discourse of its singular plural. For the plurality of the arts must
finally make perceptible a fundamental double law.

1. By touching on presentation itself, or on patency, one touches
on nothing, one does not penetrate a secret; one touches on
obviousness, and the obviousness is such that one cannot be done
with it, that it multiplies itself in its very immanence: color,
nuance, grain, line, timbre, echo, cadence . . .

2. As soon as it takes place, "art" vanishes; it is *an* art, the latter is
a work, which is *a* style, a manner, a mode of resonance with other
sensuous registers, a rhythmic reference back through indefinite
networks. In a certain very precise sense, art itself is in essence
nonapparent and/or disappearing. It even disappears twice: its
unity syncopates itself in material plurality. (The moment of the
Kantian sublime or that of the Hegelian dissolution is always
present, at work *in* aesthetic "immanence" itself.)

That is also why we are not seeking a "definition," a "determination," or even a "description" of art, which we would then be
hoping to renew on the basis of the plurality of the arts. We are
seeking merely a fashion of not leaving this diversity behind, a

fashion not of "saying" but of *articulating* something of "art,"
singular plural, right at its inorganic plurality and without synthesis or without system.

What is more, this should not make way for any aestheticism.
What is called aestheticism always has its seed or its primary
condition in a tendentious assumption of "Art" in the singular. No
doubt the aesthetic, in the sense of an aestheticism, always risks
covering over what is at stake, inasmuch as the singular of "art" is
not without its own consistency, since it *consists* in its own plural.
No doubt a religion of art always risks fastening a sacred respect on
the "work" there where one should only look to (look at) its
operation, which is to say also its *technique*. The technicity of art
dislodges art from its "poetic" assurance, if one understands by that
the production of a revelation, or art conceived as a *phusis* unveiled
in its truth. Technicity *itself* is also the "out-of-workness" [*dé-
soeuvrement*] of the work, what puts it outside itself, touching the
infinite. Their technical out-of-workness incessantly *forces* the fine
arts, dislodges them endlessly from aestheticizing repose. This is
also why art is always *coming to its end*. The "end of art" is always
the beginning of its plurality. It could also be the beginning of
another sense of and for "technics" in general.[64]

"Technique" is a rule for an end. When the end is in-finite, the
rule must conform. In a sense, this is a summary of thinking about
art since romanticism—since the infinitization of the ends of man.
The romanticism of "art"—of absolute or total art—consists in
hypostasizing the Infinite End (Poetry, Fragment, or *Gesamtkunst-
werk*). With that, technique dissolves into the form of the "genius."
To overcome romanticism is to think rigorously the in-finite,
which is to say, its finite, plural, heterogeneous constitution. Finitude is not the deprivation but the in-finite affirmation of what
incessantly *touches* on its end: another *sense* of existence and, by the
same token, another sense of "technique."

~

In this manner, a certain determination of "art," which is ours—
in other words, that of the period that will have named "art" as

such and absolutely—is perhaps coming to its end, and with it the
categorization of the "fine arts" that accompany it, and with these a
whole aesthetic feeling and judgment, a whole sublime delectation.
It is not an end, but a renewed demand to grant rights to the naked
presentation of the singular plural of obviousness—or of existence:
it's the same thing. This is as much as to say it is a duty. It is a duty
for art to put an end to "art." But this duty does not, in some
puritan mode, erect an "ethics" against an "aesthetics." Nor does it
stem from what one would be tempted to call an "ethics of the
aesthetic." This duty utters *sense* as *ethos*.

Such a duty imposes art, or it imposes "some art"—but not Art—
as the categorical imperative of after-the-divine-creation (which is
already, although but dimly perceived, the true situation of the
Kantian imperative). This duty alone gives a content to the formal-
ism of the categorical imperative: it alone fulfills an end that is not
the form of the law, but the ground-figure of presentation or
patency. Just as art is before religion (even if this has no sense
diachronically), likewise it comes after religion: today. But it is not
Art that comes, it is the *tekhnē* of existence, for this is not *phusis*.
Its—obvious—patency is not the blooming of a rose.

Ethics is there, in the very exact sense that we do not lack moral
norms, or virtues, or values today any more than yesterday. (That
we go against them or disobey them is another matter.) But what is
lacking in this moment is the *ars* that give them sense, the *ars* of
existing—not an "art of living," but technique as relation to endless
ends.

One can try to decipher something of such an *ethos* in this poem
by the painter Kandinsky, to which all that has preceded will
perhaps have been—involuntarily—but a commentary:

SEHEN

Blaues, Blaues hob sich, hob sich und fiel.
Spitzes, Dünnes, pfiff und drängte sich ein, stach aber
    nicht durch.
An allen Ecken hats gedröhnt.
Dickbraunes blieb hängen scheinbar auf alle Ewigkeiten.

Scheinbar. Scheinbar.
Breiter sollst du deine Arme ausbreiten.
Breiter. Breiter.
Und dein Gesicht sollst du mit roten Tuch bedecken.
Und vielleicht ist es noch gar nicht verschoben: bloss du
    hast dich verschoben.
Weisser Sprung nach weissem Sprung.
Und nach diesem weissen Sprung wieder ein weisser
    Sprung.
Und in diesem weissen Sprung ein weisser Sprung. In
    jedem weissen Sprung ein weisser Sprung.
Das ist eben nicht gut, dass du das Trübe nicht siehst: im
    Trüben sitzt es ja gerade.
Daher fängt auch alles an — — —
— — — es hat gekracht.

SEEING

Blue, blue arose and fell.
Sharp, thin, whistled and penetrated, but did not pierce
    through.
Everywhere a rumbling.
Thick brown hovered seemingly for all eternity.
Seemingly. Seemingly.
Spread your arms wider.
Wider. Wider.
And cover your face with a red cloth.
And perhaps it is not yet displaced at all: only you have
    displaced yourself.
White leap after white leap.
And in this white leap a white leap. In every white leap a
    white leap.
It is not good that you fail to see the turbid: it is precisely
    in the turbid that it dwells.
And that is where everything begins—
—there was a crash.[65]

The girl who succeeds the Muses. Bearer of offerings from Pompeii. (See note 12.)

§ 2 The Girl Who Succeeds the Muses

(The Hegelian Birth of the Arts)

1. It is now well established that what has been imputed to Hegel as the declaration of an "end of art" is but the declaration of an end of what he called "aesthetic religion," that is, of art as the place where the divine appears.[1] To be sure, the religion that is thus surpassed is the Greek religion, and the one that succeeds it (allowing for the Roman episode, to which we will return), the "revealed" or Christian religion, is by rights beyond art. In this regard, art is surpassed in any case. Things are far from being as simple as all that in Hegel himself, however. In fact, although the existence of Christian art is not mentioned in *The Phenomenology of Spirit* (where, on the other hand, we find the episode of the "girl" that is going to concern us), in the *Aesthetics* this art is given an important place. It even constitutes the central moment of the lectures (the center of this center being in turn constituted by painting). In the *Aesthetics*, art is supposedly surpassed, not in revealed religion, but in philosophy or in the element of pure thought. One may even assert that, for this reason, the Christian religion remains indissociable from its art, and that along with that art it must surpass or overcome the representative moment to which it still belongs and thus it too must be surpassed, or sublated, in thought.

But—to jump right away to the result—this surpassing proves to be impossible: something, which is not properly something of religion but of art, absolutely resists absorption by the dialectical

41

spiral. In fact, the last twist of this spiral should take place in the final "dissolution" of art by *poetry*, inasmuch as the latter would exhaust in itself the law of sensible exteriorization, which is the law of art. Thus: "poetry destroys the fusion of spiritual inwardness with external existence to an extent that begins to be incompatible with the original conception of art, with the result that poetry runs the risk of losing itself in a transition from the region of sense into that of the spirit" (*A*, 2: 968). Poetry is thus the "end" of art insofar as it is an *endangering* of art. And this endangering puts in danger a necessity of the "sensible presentation" that is itself an absolute necessity of the Idea, or the truth, insofar as one and the other, one or the other, must *essentially appear*, or make themselves *felt*.

When art is endangered, it is its destination "for the senses," which we have just recalled, that is put in danger. Therefore, in spite of everything, poetry must, for Hegel, maintain itself in the logic of this destination and treat as a sensible material the very language that it tends to reduce "to a meaningless sign" of a pure inwardness: this will be its rhythmic and sonorous element. But that is not all: in the same movement, poetry will grant a place to the arts in general; it will preserve their necessity or sharpen their resistance, to the point of indicating by itself and in itself the persistence of the *differences* between the arts, which differences belong to the common "destination for the senses." Thus Hegel continues: "The beautiful mean between these extremes [spiritual inwardness and real exteriority] is occupied by sculpture, painting, and music." One may therefore say that art—attaining its extreme limit in poetry precisely because it then touches on its limit, the very limit on which Sense would come to dissolve all the senses and to be no longer perceptible—touches on its own essence and recalls it forcefully according to the "beautiful mean," which is itself triple, of its sensible or sensuous effectivity. This is why poetry, in the movement by which it "seeks the concrete" for the pure spirituality whose limit it exposes (or, in other words, at the limit of which it exposes itself), and therefore when it attempts to provoke "a strengthened sensuous impression," can do so "only by means foreign to itself and borrowed from painting and music."

The point of art's dissolution is therefore *identically* and *essentially* the point of the reaffirmation of its plastic independence and of the correlative and no less essential affirmation of the *intrinsic plurality of the moments of this sensuous, perceptible plasticity.*

That is not all: as presentation of spiritual inwardness, poetry finds itself confronted with the *prose* of thinking. This prose would therefore be, by rights, the element in which it would finally come to be dissolved, and all art and all arts with it. Everywhere in Hegel, "prose" is synonymous with non-art. But this non-art shows a singular ambiguity: it is at once the index of pure interiority withdrawn into itself, of the "pure element of thinking" that receives into itself a thoroughly sublated exteriority, and also a mode of presentation of this pure spirit. But this mode is itself merely particular, and the prose of thinking is deficient inasmuch as it is *only* thinking:

> Thinking, however, results in thought alone; it evaporates the form of reality into the form of the pure Concept, and even if it grasps and apprehends real things in their particular character and real existence, it nevertheless lifts even this particular sphere into the element of the universal and ideal wherein alone thinking is at home with itself. . . . Thinking is only a reconciliation between reality and truth within thinking itself. But poetic creation and formation is a reconciliation in the form of a *real* phenomenon itself, even if this form be presented only spiritually. (*A*, 2: 976)

Thus it can become poetry's task to take "speculative thinking into the imagination and give it a body as it were within the spirit itself" (*A*, 2: 977).[2]

2. Several indications converge, therefore, to suggest that art is again "given body," reincarnated as it were at the very limit of its own dissolution, and that in "reincarnating" itself, it again grants a place to the set of "particularizations" that are essential to it.

This amounts to saying that art is properly art—and *arts*—only when it is withdrawn from the sole service of divine presentation, and when it presents itself *as such*. Doubtless, this leaves *properly unthought*, and no doubt unthinkable, in Hegel, the "service" or the "office" that should be that of art in these conditions, if it is also not possible to designate with any precision what the "reincarnation of the speculative" or its *pure plasticity* (see n. 2) would be. Perhaps this impossibility is due to the fact that the plasticity in question cannot be "pure": if it were, it would remain in the moment of interiority; if, on the contrary, it is in exteriority, it offers interiority as a vanished or clouded interiority in the exteriority that it will itself have become . . . One of the aspects of this exteriority as such will necessarily be the plurality of its (sensuous, perceptible) "plastic" instances. But this only makes more evident the fact that there is a specifically proper moment of art, which is absolutely irreducible—and as such is doubtless necessarily balanced on its own "beautiful mean," and on the mean of this mean, which is painting, the balancing point of external multiplicity and spiritual unity.[3]

There is a moment that necessarily and essentially joins the dissolution of art, as merely exterior element of the true presentation of the Idea, to the presentation of art, as sensuous destination of truth. In religious terms, the moment preceding this moment is the religion of the divine that is simply present in the beautiful form, whereas the succeeding moment is the religion of the divine incarnate up to and including the death of sensuous, perceptible manifestation. *But in terms of art*, these preceding and succeeding moments themselves appear and appear only as the proper and autonomous sphere of art, which is also and in the same movement the sphere of the diverse arts in their necessary particularization. The preceding moment is the (technical) artistic moment of "form," the succeeding moment is the no less artistic and technical moment of *the form of the decomposition of merely formal presence*.

The passage from the one into the other, which is itself as much a vanishing as an appearing, is represented in a very precise manner when, in *The Phenomenology of Spirit*, Hegel has us witness the transmission down to the present of works of antique art detached from the spiritual life that was theirs. This transmission accompanies the movement through which aesthetic religion, as a result of its negation in the Roman world, begins its sublation into revealed religion. Considered for itself, which is how the text demands to be read, the transmission remains apart from this process: it is added to it or subtracted from it, as one prefers, but it installs properly at this juncture the irreducible, unsublatable insistence of art.

Here is the text:

Trust in the eternal laws of the gods has vanished, and the Oracles, which pronounced on particular questions, are dumb. The statues are now cadavers from which the living soul has flown, just as hymns are words from which belief has gone. The tables of the gods provide no spiritual food and drink, and consciousness no longer recovers, in games and festivals, the joyful unity of itself with the essence. The works of the Muse now lack the power of the Spirit, for the Spirit has gained its certainty of itself from the crushing of gods and men. They have become what they are for us now—beautiful fruit already picked from the tree, which a friendly Fate has offered us, as a girl might set the fruit before us. There is neither the actual life in which they existed, nor the tree that bore them, nor the earth and elements which constituted their substance, nor the climate which gave them their peculiar character, nor the cycle of the changing seasons that governed the process of their growth. So Fate does not restore their world to us along with the works of antique Art, it gives not the spring and summer of the ethical life in which they blossomed and ripened, but only the veiled recollection of that actual world. Our active enjoyment of them is therefore not an act of divine worship through which our consciousness might come to its perfect truth and fulfilment; it is an external activity—the wiping-off of some drops of rain or specks of dust from these fruits, so to speak—one which erects an intricate scaffolding of the dead elements of their outward existence—the language, the historical circumstances, etc. in place of the inner elements of the ethical life which environed, created, and inspired them. And all this we do, not in order to enter into their very life but only to possess an idea of them in our imagination. But, just as the girl who offers us the plucked fruits is more than their nature—their conditions and elements, the tree, air, light, etc.—which directly provided them—

because she sums all this up in a higher mode, in the gleam of her self-conscious eye and in the gesture of offering, so, too, the Spirit of the Fate that presents us with those works of art is more than the ethical life and the actual world of that nation, for it is the *inwardizing recollection* in us of the Spirit which was still *exalienated* in them; it is the Spirit of the tragic Fate which gathers all those individual gods and attributes of substance into one Pantheon, into the Spirit that is itself conscious of itself as Spirit. (*PS*, 455–56)[4]

It is therefore clear that works of art—which have only *become* these "works" as such, and been deposited in our memories as in the museum, this new site of the Muses—are no longer presented except as "cadavers," forever deprived of the divine life that animated them. Thus, their interiority is empty, but to the extent that it was an interiority as yet only "exalienated" (purely exteriorized) in them, in their forms, it finds itself in turn "interiorized" by the "consciousness" of what this interiority demands, and it is thus prepared for the birth of the Spirit in the exteriority, which is itself interiorizing, of the human person of the son of the unique God.

In this regard, the girl looks like a kind of angel who leads the gathered figures of Antiquity toward the divine birth in the manger. But this movement of interiority does not simply reduce the side of exteriority: the works are at the same time "presented" and "offered" as such. In this other regard, then, the girl is the founder and the guardian of the museum. Entering into the museum, the works also become properly "the works of the Muses." Detached from the tree, the soil, and the climate, they become properly "these beautiful fruits," which now put forth only the value of their beauty. The offering of this beauty is the act of a "friendly" fate, that is, of a fate that did not let what was surpassed pass away without also gathering up from it the element or the aspect of it that we still "enjoy," or rather, by which we now properly take joy in this sensuous beauty as such. The fruits are dead, because detached, but this death preserves for them an inalterable sensuousness. More than that, since "self-consciousness" and "the gesture of offering" together make up the posture of the "girl," one might say that the spiritual interiorization goes hand in hand with the unilateral exteriorization according to which the works of the Muses appear in effect as the reverse of spiritual memory, as an immemorial fixing in place of simple sensuous appearance, which knows nothing any longer of what it presented but which, by being itself presented, would present in immobility the pure and obscure necessity of sensuous exteriority to itself.

3. Who, then, is this girl? First of all, what is the fate from which she comes and of which she is the figure?

This fate is the fate of religion. It is so in the form of the fate, in itself torn and contradictory, of Hegelian (which is to say, Christian) religion, for such religion is in no sense an immediate relation of a divine person to a human person; it is the mediated development of infinite subjectivity that reveals itself insofar as it goes out of itself in order to return to itself. In this manner, the Hegelian element of religion is constituted by an intimate and infinite fragility: it is, in effect, divided from the beginning between the becoming for-itself of the Absolute (pure thought) and the irreducibly sensuous manifestation of this same becoming. In a certain way, religion has nothing here that is truly proper to it, and it tends to be nothing other than the untenable, undecidable line of cleavage between art and philosophy.[5]

Hegel could thus, in a late text, place art and philosophy together in the same relation to religion, a relation obviously that of a true freedom to a relative submission. As we will see, Hegel presents as a "secret" this thesis, according to which the "end of art" (religious art) is identical to the liberation of art (artistic art).

"Art makes its appearance with philosophy and religion. Fine and free art presents itself at the same time as philosophy or even a little earlier, when the real, healthy life of nations no longer finds satisfaction in its existence. Art also has its end in the ideal. It is thus that Greek art flourished at the same time as the philosophy of art. When life no longer suffices, one creates for oneself an ideal realm. . . . The intelligible world of philosophy is simply more abstract than the ideal world of art. Thus we see in the fifteenth century, at the moment of the transformation and disappearance of the feudal world, art appearing freely for itself. Art seems to be a means of promoting [*eine Beförderung*] religion; yet its position in relation to religion is secretly the same as that of philosophy. Its aim is that man should produce, by drawing them from his own source, *other formations* than religion, ones which must be more satisfying for the human spirit than those that religiosity offers him."[6] In sum, art, religion, and philosophy appear together when simple living immediacy comes undone. But art and philosophy are both the double *free* form of the ideal, its abstract side and its concrete side, whereas religion remains the formation that is both merely intermediary and not free of the same ideal.

∽

The complexity and the difficulty of the relations between art and religion can be found throughout their double history. Art as such appears with the Egyptian religion, that is, with the overcoming of the moment in which the spirit is always present in the totality. (This refers in particular to the Hindu religion.) "The difference lies in whether the different moments or aspects are regarded as pertaining to the essence or not" (*PR*, 374). If they do belong to it, then "the way in which [God] manifests himself and becomes apparent in his determinate being is determined from within," and it is at this moment that "the need to portray God through fine art arises" (*PR*, 374). This is the moment of "the birth of art" insofar as "the sensible [mode of] determinate being, in which the deity is intuited, corresponds to the concept of the deity; it is not a sign but gives expression at every point to the fact that it is produced from within, and corresponds fully to the thought or inner concept. But the essential point is that this determinate being is still a mode of sensible visibility" (*PR*, 376).

Because this sensuous intuition is not yet the very being of the god posing itself outside, but simply the positioning of a being by a separate subjectivity, "the work of art is produced by human hands" (*PR,* 376),[7] and here art means first of all technics. But this technics contains in itself a determining moment of art: before beauty in the proper sense, non-submission to naturality, the freedom of production.

This trait of *artificial* production is also the first determining trait of aesthetic religion (between the two, there will have been the moment, which is Jewish, of the "religion of sublimity" in which "God has become the god of free men" existing "for itself, in its image"). Then the "existence of the spirit is a work of art," that is, an external, natural reality, to which is given the "appearance of freedom." Here technics has become *poiēsis,* and the Greek gods, as beautiful sensuous apparitions, are themselves the products of *poiēsis.* Progress in the expression of divine essence is necessarily mediated by the progress of free human subjectivity or self-consciousness, and though the god aroused the desire for art, at present men as artists "make or shape their God for themselves" (*PR,* 475). "Hence the gods of the Greeks are products of human imagination or sculptured [*plastisch*] deities formed by human hands. They originate therefore in a finite manner, one produced by poets, by the Muse" (*PR,* 657). "Thus God is something made by human beings. Poets, sculptors, and painters taught the Greeks what their gods were" (*PR,* 659, n. 412). The Greek gods "are made or poetically created [*gedichtet*], but they are not fictitious [*erdichtet*]. To be sure, they emerge from human phantasy in contrast with what is already at hand, but they emerge as essential shapes" (*PR,* 658, n. 409).

Hegel's "religion of beauty" can therefore be considered in two ways. From one angle, it is the religion in which the divine is presented according to the ideality of its presence, as "essential shape"; in this respect, it remains caught up in ideality or is ignorant of "genuine ideality," that is, the ideality for which manifestation must proceed to immediate reality, present in the form of this one, this man (Christ), this self-consciousness. That is why the statue, when it becomes a "cadaver," has lost the merely ideal or essential divinity that it presented and cannot be resuscitated like Christ, in whom ideality traverses negativity. But from another angle, beauty subsists as the moment proper to "the genius of art externalizing the revelation of the divine content," inasmuch as this moment is not an externalization such that the spirit is lost in it until it finds itself resuscitated, that is, reinternalized; rather, spirit (the divine) remains there outside itself since it is "not God who has being for himself, but only itself the implicit being of being-for-self, being-for-other as such. This includes both explicit and implicit being but without mediation, as an abstract result to which mediation is extraneous. So the side of determinate being does not go so far as to make the god (as work of art) self-knowledge; knowledge is extraneous to him and pertains to the human, subjective spirit" (*PR*, 476, n. 626).

The un-conscious and in-animate exteriority of the work of art, which constitutes strictly the element of beauty, is thus what remains when the gods have disappeared in this form, and *this remainder, as such,* is also the sustained moment, subsisting by itself, of the "in-itself" which has its mediation entirely outside itself. This could also be translated as follows: art is the truth of religion from the side of exteriority as nonrevealed exteriority in interiority (and philosophy is the symmetrical truth from the side of interiority). One may thus conclude that religion has no absolutely proper truth—but also that art, as its "exterior" truth, is not the art "in service" of religion, but precisely the art which is only art, which has its truth as such.

This is why, in the same context, when Hegel wants to indicate how the Christian religion will overcome the moment of beautiful ideality, he finds himself paradoxically constrained to grant Christian art a beauty for which, in principle, it has no use (or more exactly, he finds himself constrained to recall Christian art, when he could have kept silent about it, as in the *Phenomenology*): "This Greek ideality could not occur at any subsequent time. Certainly the art of the Christian religion is beautiful but ideality is not its ultimate principle" (*PR*, 660, n. 412). This "certainly" says it all:

either this art is beautiful, and ideality—in the sense of the independence of the form—is also its principle, or else it is not beautiful, and it is not art, and it dissolves itself.

The moment of art in religion cannot, therefore, remain a moment. Irresistibly it autonomizes itself, and it does so, perhaps, because it is precisely the moment of the thorough autonomy of manifestation—of an autonomy that no longer retains anything of interiority or of spirituality as such. Art would thus behave like a sort of "sublation in exteriority" of religion—but since religion has its truth only in the return of the spirit to itself, art is also the definitive alienation of the religious, which also might be expressed thus: the technics of the beautiful, or better still, the beautiful as technics in (the) place of divine presence.

This is what would come to be offered with the "girl." She is Roman. The only possibility, in fact, of assigning a reference to this enigmatic character is to see in her one of the figures of Pompeii, which Hegel knew.[8] These figures of young girls are bearers of offerings in the cults. Nevertheless, they do not signify, in the Hegelian scheme, a return of the religious. Rather, one must consider that Roman religion is the religion "of purposiveness" in which the "gods" are not valorized by their presence, but by the protection and services one may expect of them. The Roman spirit "is more perfectly at home in the finite and in what is immediately useful," in the name of which it invokes divine powers reduced to a "prosaic" condition, that is, one from which "all determination of divinity disappears" (*PR*, 382–83). The prosaic and self-consciousness are the two features of the Roman element in which all divine spirituality tends to vanish. In a sense, art itself vanishes—except by maintaining there, despite everything, the moment of pure form, so purely formal that it is entirely in the exteriority of grace and charm: the girl, whose offering is no longer interpreted by Hegel as a cultic offering but as the offering of the "works of the Muses" in their simple detached exteriority. The girl is in effect the self-consciousness of art *both* as gathered consciousness of divine interiority that is going to become "the spirit conscious of itself as spirit"—that is, the man-God—*and* as consciousness of art as art.

4. Just as she is the representative of a cult in which religion gets "damaged," the girl also belongs to an art that begins to lose itself by proceeding "in its *content* to completing the process of individualization and its contingency, in its *form* to the agreeable and the attractive" (*A*, 1: 500). Thus, the "seriousness of the gods becomes a gracefulness which does not agitate a man or lift him above his particular character but lets him remain at peace in it and claims only to please him" (ibid.). Nevertheless, the isolation of the sole moment of pleasure, grace, and charm must also be considered as in some sense the final or perfect isolation of the moment of art and of form as such. For it is indeed in art that "pleasure and enjoyment are justified and sanctified" (*A*, 1: 78): one is to understand by this that artistic "sanctification" is not of the order of a "divine service," but that the "saintliness" in question takes place only in art, as art, and right at it (or them).

Doubtless, Greek art in general finds its exhaustion in Rome, that is, it confesses there, in the end, the lack of inwardness of the "plastic Ideal" (*A*, 1: 504) as such. For this reason, revealed religion will have a content "which art did not invent" (*A*, 2: 505), and the possibility of its coming will have been prepared by the fundamental prosaic nature of Rome, where "we find no beautiful, free, and great art" (*A*, 1: 514). But the girl turns out to have at her disposal an attribute that, without elevating her above simple grace and the pure plasticity of her offering stance, gives her the brilliance of interiority all the same: it is the brilliance of her eye. This brilliance was lacking in the statues of Greece: "The expression of the soul in its simplicity, namely the light of the eye, is absent from the sculptures. The supreme works of beautiful sculpture are sightless, and their inner being does not look out of them as self-knowing inwardness in this spiritual concentration which the eye discloses. . . . But the God of romantic art appears seeing" (*A*, 1: 520–21).

Thus the girl of the *Phenomenology*, transported into the *Aesthetics*, constitutes this infinitely complex figure in which ancient art is both immobilized and transported into the element of Christian art, in which the gaze is lit up in the presentation of gazeless forms, in which inwardness shines and offers itself gracefully, without, however, offering anything other than its grace.[9] A figure that seems to be nothing other than a rhetorical figure for illustrating a "friendly Fate" is revealed (without revealing anything) as being *secretly* the unique plastic figure of an art that is barely worthy of the name art, but this form has *secretly* the power to preserve, in spite of all religion either past or to come, an irreducible, indisputable exigency of sensuous form.

It has not been said, it has been kept secret, that the girl has her provenance in art: she behaves like the concrete and contingent individuality of the son of man who would be God, pure spirit. But everything points to the fact that her silhouette is in effect copied from an album; it is an engraving whose line, quickly effaced, traverses or pierces for an instant the page of writing. She is herself a technique of writing whereby one is made to touch the fruits that no discourse can touch.

A form turns out to represent nothing; it puts nothing into form except the graceful consistency of the form itself. A form turns out to be "in itself," without mediation, the "for-itself" of the "spirit" it is lacking. But if it lacks "spirit," its consciousness and its certainty are in the fruits she presents, in the gesture of her presentation, and in the brilliance of an eye that is nothing other than one of the fruits, or rather, the brilliance of their beauty. For to the extent that art "has to convert every shape in all points of its visible surface into an eye, which is the seat of the soul and brings the spirit into appearance," the painting of the eye is itself the quintessence of painting, the painting of painting and the painting of art itself. In fact, "painting is not concerned with making visible as such but with the visibility which is both self-particularizing and also inwardized . . . in painting, the material . . . is lit up in itself and precisely on this account itself darkens the light" (*A*, 2: 626).[10] But in this way the subject matter in painting is nothing other than subjectivity itself, which "is the spiritual light lit up from within itself" (*A*, 2: 846).

The eye of the girl—and the gesture it lights up, by which it is lit up in its turn—this presented eye of presentation is nothing less than *entirely exposed interiority*, but at the point at which it no longer even refers to itself as to some content or some latent presence, having become on the contrary *the patency of its very latency* and thus irreconcilable with any interiority (with any divinity).

5. For this reason, the girl who is at once the infinitely fragile extremity of art and the infinitely tenuous passage of beautiful form in the transformation of form into truth—this girl has no other existence than that of the fruits she presents. For this to occur, she cannot be the gathering together of their brilliance in the concentration of a gaze without being identically the multiplication of her inconsistent identity into the plurality, which is alone consistent and preserved, of the works of the Muses.

This is not a unity or a negative identity. It is much more, and much more immobile, and much more open, than a dialectical process. In the infinite movement of the gesture of presentation, dialectical logic is interrupted: spirit is not going to reengender itself in greater conformity with its pure spirituality by hollowing out its negativity. The gesture suspends this movement. By suspending it, the gesture interrupts the sense of the dialectic, but it presents the form: the *Präsentieren* that is the sole office of the girl. By interrupting the sense, the gesture interrupts religion, and in this way it interrupts art conceived as the derived, external, and unseeing expression of the internal gaze of pure presence. But by presenting the form, by presenting itself as a gesture of presentation without interiority, without any other secret than the very diversity of works, with the minute grace of a fugitive figure it gives one to see this gesture alone: a life that consents to the suspension of sense, and consequently to the infinite diversity of elaborations [*mises en oeuvre*], of which each one is this gesture itself, but of which none reveals the sense, because all in all the revealed, the truth, is the gesture itself.[11]

Thus, the girl exposes art that consents to its own disappearance:

not in order to be resuscitated but because it does not enter into that process. The "beautiful fruits" are detached from the tree, and their presentation is the consenting to this being-detached, mortally immortal. What if art were never anything but the necessarily plural, singular art of consenting to death, of consenting to existence?

Caravaggio, *The Death of the Virgin*, 1605–6.
Louvre Museum, Paris.

§ 3 On the Threshold

For Marie-Eve Druette

So, we have entered there where we will never enter, into this scene painted on a canvas. All at once, there we are. We can't exactly say that we have penetrated there, but neither can we say that we are outside. We are there in a manner older and simpler than by any movement, displacement, or penetration. We are there without leaving the threshold, on the threshold, neither inside nor outside—and perhaps we are, ourselves, the threshold, just as our eye conforms to the plane of the canvas and weaves itself into its fabric.

∿

On the threshold, all at once, a scene stands out. This scene is not staged for us, it is not laid out for the attention or the intention of a subject. Everything happens in an indifference to the visitor, and it even seems that it ought to remain hidden from whoever is not, already, one of a familiar circle. No one looks at us or invites us in. Indiscreet, we have, in sum, entered by force. But this force of intrusion is that of the scene itself. If one dared, one might say that it ravishes us. In any case, we are seized there, on the spot, in our very discretion. This force seizes and carries off on the spot, as in a transport of the place that would be nothing other than place itself, without inside or outside—nothing but the flattening of a plane.

We are seized there, carried off in the rise or violent flaring up of a drapery; we are projected into an oblique spurt of light that bends the pates toward the face of the reclining woman, before it splashes back toward us by means of the brilliance of an offered nape, and then ends in the reflection of a copper basin. Here, at our feet, already overflowing the frame, the orange-colored oval of the basin, along with that of the dress that repeats it, gives us our place on the threshold: we close the circle, or perhaps the ellipsis, of the assembled presences around the one who lies there and the one who grieves. We "compear" [*comparaissons*] with these presences.

～

At what are we thus present or to what are we presented? To what are we exposed? Everything shows us that it is death. It is the very thing shown to us, painted for us: Here, you are on the threshold of death. The scene is carried off not in an ascending movement but in a heavy fall, on the order of the double fold of drapery that falls down in sharp points, a double arrow, beak, or index pointed at the bare feet of the dead woman whose dress, in turn, cloth of the same shade, falls toward the floor beneath the stretcher or crude bed.

Its thick wooden feet, like those of the chair, repeat at floor level the heavy, squared-off structure of the beam and the joists of the ceiling. Everything is weighed down in this closed room, as if mortised and pinioned from top to bottom, plane against plane; everything is overwhelmed, everyone is overtaken by grief. Even the light itself falls.

The source of daylight in this room will remain out of sight, whereas its difficult traversal or passage through the penumbra divides the bare wall with a diagonal that crosses the falling fold of the curtain. Together, the light and the fold give the pattern or rhythm to what has come to pass, in other words, to this: that it is passing, that it is becoming lost in the shadow or right at the ground, at our feet, and that what is lit up is obscurity itself, what is presented is absencing, carrying off [*l'absentement, l'enlèvement*].

～

She did not die here. They have carried her to this makeshift bed where they deposited her body, slackened in a posture not yet arranged, to wash it before the funeral. Her hands have not been placed in a manner that would imitate prayer. Someone has just pulled back the covering in which she had been wrapped. The body and the face are swollen, the hair is undone, the bodice unlaced. It is said that the painter took for a model a woman drowned in the Tiber. It is also said that she appeared to be suffering from dropsy. Water is perhaps the secret element or prism of this scene bathed in tears. The water or oil of the painting, that which washes, that which flows or streams, spreads and permeates, swells and scents, the ablution, dissolution, suspension, and floating. And yet, this body is firm, whole, intact in its abandon.

It is not here that this woman died, but here she is not exactly dead. One might also say she is resting, as if she were still on this side of death, or else already beyond it. But is not death itself already both on this side and beyond death?

And is it not for this reason that there is not, there is never "death *itself*"?

And what if that were the subject of this painting: there is never death "itself"? What if that were its subject, its support, its substance, its stuff, and its secret? That there is not "death," but a dead man, a dead woman, numerous dead who are firm, whole, present among us, woven with us into life, into its stuff and its secret?

∽

Let us not, however, seek to go behind the canvas; rather than trying to see behind the visible, let us not seek anything other than the brief immobilization of the oil. We have entered, already; we are exposed to seeing; that is all we are asked, that is all we are permitted, and that is all we are promised. By a device which is far from being unique in painting, but which here finds one of its chosen places, the canvas signals to us, makes us this sign: Enter and look. Come and see. Exhaust your looks until your eyes close, until your hands are raised over them, until your faces fall upon your knees. See the invisible. This is the ordinary command or demand of painting: very simple, very humble, even derisory. See the invisible, not beyond the visible, nor inside, nor outside, but right at it, on the threshold, like its very oil, its weave, and its pigment.

The painting, then, lights up here only one look: that of the closed eyes of the dead woman on whose eyelids all of the light falls. Right away it spreads out all around, but it also invades this whole body. The woman's body radiates the light; it is light shed, abandoned, shining for no other world than for itself, for its own body, for its own skin of light, and for its own purple cloth. A woman, a face, a throat, hands, but yet another woman, her nape, her cheek, her hand.

They hold each other, answer each other, the one thrown back and the other thrown forward, the one showing her face, the other her back, linked by a whiteness of cloth, from the sheet to the bodice, from the shroud to the shift. Everything here is woven in cloth.

The one appears to support the other, bent like a caryatid beneath the bust and the swollen belly of the dead woman. The other appears to surround the first in her wide open arm, to bring her into the light. They answer each other across the two shores of death, and between them there is not death itself; there is nothing but light and the thin line of shadow that runs along the edges of the bodies, the folds of the linen and the clothes.

The one the other woman, before beyond death. Neither life nor another life, but the brightness of their alternate presences, from the breast of the one to the shoulder of the other, from the inside of the one to the outside of the other.

~

If there is not death itself, neither is there before nor beyond. Death: we are never there, we are always there. Inside and outside, at once, but without communication between inside and outside, without mixture, without mediation, and without crossing. Perhaps that is what we have access to here, as to that which is absolutely inaccessible. Perhaps it is to this that we ourselves are the access, we mortals. Perhaps that is the water, the light, and the stuff of this visibility. The very thing, the threshold that we are, we the living. The very plane, plan, or ground of the canvas, in every sense of these words. The large drapery like our eyelid, not a veil that unveils, not a revelation, but the power and the intention to see carried off, stretched, and folded right into the cloth, which is to say right into the stuff of the cloth [*l'étoupe*], the material that fills out and, with a same light, sustains the look and stifles it.

From the inside of (the) painting to the outside of (the) painting, there is nothing, no passage. There is painting, there is us, indistinctly, distinctly. Here, (the) painting is our access to the fact that we do not accede—either to the inside or to the outside of ourselves. Thus we exist. This painting paints the threshold of existence. In these conditions, to paint does not mean to represent, but simply to pose the ground, the texture, and the pigment of the threshold.

~

If it is a question here of death, it is more on the side of these men. The most visible among them are very old. The light harshly isolates three bald skulls. The group they form barely leaves the shadow; it remains immobile, a stranger to the rhythm of the two women, of their bodies and the red cloths. The group of men sustains the shadow; rather than extracting itself from the darkness, the group is the plural form of the shadow. The men form the other threshold; they are inside what we are outside. But between the dress and the drapery, it is as if a monstrous jaw opened on this people of shadow, to vomit them or swallow them.

With their long tunics falling straight along the plane of the canvas, they are all, all eleven of them, death "itself," which is to say, they are not. They are not, all together, no more than they are one by one, being all alike, as we are and as they are like us, figures and colors quickly drowned in the indistinct background, our fellow men, our neighbors—except perhaps the one who is dreaming directly above the luminous face. He alone, younger than the rest, seems to be remembering something other than their bony and frozen grief.

So who is he? Why not begin the necessary interlude of representation or of signification with him?

He is John the Apostle, the beloved disciple, the one whom so many painters have painted with the grace of a woman. These men are the Apostles, and the dead woman is the Virgin, and the other woman is Mary Magdalene. This painting was commissioned for an Unshod Carmelite church in Rome, where it was supposed to represent the Dormition of the Virgin, or her *transito*, her passage into heaven. But it was rejected—*fu levata via*, says the history book—and the Duke of Mantua bought it on the advice of the painter Rubens. The reasons for this rejection have remained partly obscure. Historians and commentators clear things up more or less as follows. Caravaggio, here much more than elsewhere, had dismissed the sacredness, glory, and royalty of the Virgin in the imminence of her Assumption. No opening onto heaven or onto her throne, no angels ready to carry off Mary. The painter had transformed the supernatural scene into a popular one. His model might have been a drowned woman, but also a prostitute, one of his mistresses, to whom he conceded visibly no more than the thinness of an evanescent halo. This was no longer a dormition, or a *transito*, passage and access to the other life; it was a vulgar death.

Yet a wholly other, religious commentary is possible and has been offered. Caravaggio would be bearing witness here to a new, profoundly human spirituality of his age (unknown to the Carmelites), which hails in Mary the co-redeemer of the most humble existence. To that end, far from painting her "without decorum," as others had written, he gave her the very pose of Christ on the cross, while by means of her swollen body beneath the purple robe, he indicates the womb that carried the Savior. With the basin, the linen, and the bare feet (which are also those of the Unshod Carmelites), he recalls the foot-washing, as does Mary Magdalene in the foreground. Washed feet are purified and they give passage from one world to the other.

Because the literature on this subject is so abundant, it would be pointless to give more than this lapidary summary of it. Naturally, the interpretations do not cancel each other out. Surely the canvas contains all these representations at once, as well as still others—for example, one might imagine a more modern interpretation that would set out from the peaceful hysteria of that womb.

~

But one must—it is only right—leave off representation and interpretation as much as possible. One must remain right at the surface of the canvas, glued to it, on its threshold. Let's come back to Saint John. Caravaggio must have known that the Antiphon of the Introit for the Mass of the Assumption is drawn from John's Apocalypse. Here is the text: "And there appeared a great wonder in heaven; a woman clothed with the sun, and the moon under her feet, and upon her head a crown of twelve stars."

John has come away from the others and turned back toward them. His left hand is just above Mary's face, like a point of inflection, reflection, or reverberation for all the light of the painting. He is thinking, he is the thought of the painting. Between red cloth and red cloth, a thought stretched like a thread.

Besides their color, the robe and the curtain have in common the presence of a cord or a lace, each time unknotted, unlaced, barely holding back the cloth. The clothing might bare the breast, the drapery might fall down onto the scene. The thought remains suspended, between knotting and unknotting. Signs are disassociated, disassembled. As one can remark here and there on the canvas, the weave is bare, which is what the painter wished. The eye touches on the underside of the paint, on its support, its subject, its substance, and its cloth or stuff.

John has come away from the others and he is considering them more than he is looking at the woman. Like him, these men come from afar: their clothing is in the ancient style, whereas the women are dressed in the Roman fashion of the time. These men sojourn in religion's past and in painting's past. They have advanced only to the threshold of the present, as we have done for our part, coming from another kind of past. They do not pass over the threshold in their faded tunics and their hieratic postures. Behind them, they have a bare wall, without pictures or ornaments. They, the apostles, carriers of epistles, announcers of gospels, they no longer have any message. Or else the only news they bring is that the message is past.

Here, there is no message and no passage. Between John and the two Marys, there is only a present of light, color, cloth, and body.

~

This quadruple present is gathered up on Mary's lips. No other part of the canvas is more carefully drawn than this mouth: this minuscule vertical line draws taut the whole top of the painting. The mouth makes the initiating stroke and the trace of the whole painting. And first of the figure that is literally the only one in the picture. A figure that does not represent, that does not identify, that is not exemplary, that is only what it is: the infinitely singular manner in which a traced line configures by virtue of no other essence than the inimitable existence of its singularity. An existence immediately lost, a model abandoned, a mold overturned.

The overturned or upturned figure offers up the lips, which are emphasized still more by the very visible nostrils and by the somewhat heavy crease of the chin. What is modeled with so much care is a heaviness, an abandon, and a waiting.

These lips do not speak. They respond to the whole lifting up of the immense curtain. They respond to it in the manner in which, to use classical painting terms, the "flesh tints" [*carnations*]—that is, the visible parts of bodies—respond to the fabrics [*étoffes*]. *Étoffes* and *carnations*, that is this whole painting in two words, and in this sense, it has nothing to do with the question of the veil, nor with that of the incarnation. No mystery here—the mystery is past. Instead, the texture and the tint of these obvious facts, still life and *tableau vivant*, and yet neither one nor the other.

~

So the model for Mary would have been a pleasure-girl [*une fille de plaisir*]—*meretrice, cortigiane*, insists the history book—who had probably slept with the painter. Even if this fact is not altogether certain, there is no doubt that the other Mary is a prostitute. She is the model whore, but in what sense must we understand that here?

Whatever may have been the real circumstances, the painter's model will not have been the Mother of God, Queen of Heaven, and if the model was also not a pleasure-girl, at least it was a girl's pleasure.

But it is no less certain that Mary the Virgin is the model of Mary the Sinner and the Penitent, she who washes Christ's feet with perfume then dries them with her hair, the same hair that is here carefully braided. This gallant hairstyle shines softly among the copperish reflections in the foreground, very close to us, touching us. In place of the royal diadem that should have been placed on the other woman, this braid is the only ornament of the canvas.

Mary is the model of Mary, and here the reversibility is endless. Each is like the outside of the other, or like her inside, simultaneously, alternatively. Each is the fabric or carnation of the other. It is no longer possible to know which is the mother of the god and which the pleasure-girl—where is sainthood, where is pleasure. But this is not a specular play. The one does not see herself in the other. Rather they exchange the absences of their gazes. And just as one imagines the tears of the one, one imagines the joy of the other. This imperceptible joy is all that passes in the vicinity of death, beside it, neither within nor without.

∼

There is neither resurrection nor assumption. There is more and less than a negotiation or a philosophy of death. There is neither abyss, nor ecstasy, nor salvation. There is pleasure and pain, which touch each other without joining, are opposed without tearing each other apart. All the hands here, held, held out, laid on, like light feeling its way about in multiple ways.

Mary is the model of Mary, but no figure is common to them both. Doubtless they together refer to a third, who, however, is not or is just barely a figure. The one and the other are a new Eve, the one according to the birth of man, the other according to his fall, a double coming into the world, fabric and carnation.

In the "Entombment" by the same painter, the two Marys are side by side, bending their heads in the same way, and Mary Magdalene wears the same dress and the same hairstyle as here. Here, however, the Virgin has gotten younger and conforms to the other Mary, the other half of Eve.

Or rather: there is not just one Eve. Eve is at least two Eves, Mary and Mary. Mary-Eve, twice, on one side and the other of death, which has no borders. The undone cords and laces are also serpents, as is the braid. Caravaggio painted a "Madonna with Serpent," which was also accused of lacking dignity.

∼

Eve, Hawwah: Adam gave this name to woman because it means "the living one." Genesis says: "because she was the mother of all living things." Eve is the life of life, which can be understood to mean pleasure as well as death. It is understood as it divides. Woman is that which divides itself.

It is not salvation, it is not redemption. There is nothing, here, to redeem. There is not, in fact, the religion of the Assumption, which is an extreme of idolatry in the religion of Redemption. No idolatry, no religion, no divine service of painting. But it is painting that can lay hold of the idol in order to turn the icon into a luminous image and convert the image into fabric and carnation. With a single gesture, this painting practices iconoclasm and the present of the image, *aphanisis* and phenomenon. It undoes semblances and causes to appear and compear fellow creatures [*semblables*]: Mary-Eve and Eve-Mary, and us, and us again, we mortals, we the living.

This is not the "Salve Regina" that the Carmelites were expecting, but it is the well-known salutation: *Ave, Eva.* Salutation/salvation [*salut*] through the reversibility of the woman's name, by its dispropriation, its putting outside/inside. A salutation/salvation that is itself reversible: *ave* engraved on a tomb meant "farewell" just as it meant "hello" in everyday language.

Here, now, a new Eve is weeping by the side of another, who is taking her leave or taking pleasure. But the lips of the other kiss that surface of which we form the threshold. A painting places its lips on ours and says "hello, farewell" to light, to presence.

~

Light, presence: what in another language one might name the open. It is to the open that we have no access because the open itself is the access to all that is. Presence is not a form or a consistency of Being; it is access. Light is not a phenomenon, but the limit-speed of the world, that of all appearance and of all exposition.

Light is the "hello, farewell," the salutation/salvation to which we do not accede because it is access. Access is not a procession, it is not an orifice: it is an expanse, a zone, a plane. It is the closed mouth, like the concentration, the hearth, the touch of the whole canvas. The mouth as the taste of the entire canvas.

If we accede, we are in the taste, in the pleasure or displeasure.

Taste is flattered or it is offended by a clash [*heurté*]. This painting clashed with the spiritual taste of the Carmelites. It does not, however, flatter a taste for death. It stands elsewhere, it flatters and clashes otherwise. To flatter is to smooth and level out a surface, to arrange the area—the Germanic *flat* or the Greek *platus*. This painting arranges and exposes its plane. It lays it out flat. To clash is to strike one's head against, like a ram. Here, several heads clash with the plane of the canvas, or else these heads are the clash of the canvas itself. But Mary's mouth flatters and clashes at the same time. The lips of the one and the braids of the other, the immense drapery and the meager cloth draped over the edge of the basin.

~

Ave responds to the Greek *khaire*, "rejoice," which also is used for farewell as well as for greeting. Rejoice, Eve, you who are the name of joy, or let us rejoice in the name of joy—that is, in the name of the fact that joy has no name, that it reduces all names, turns each of them into a greeting hurled beyond names, on this side of names. The place of the name is the place of death. But here, inside/outside, there is something else: not the loss of this world, nor death to this world, nor the assumption within the Name, but rather death in this world, as its weave, its water, its fabric, and its carnation.

Here, come in and see. To see the dead in this world, to see their bodies in this place, without painting life in the colors of death. That would be to paint without religion, to paint with the colors of painting.

Something other than death—and yet nothing other, and consequently death itself, in a sense. But this sense has no sense. An other than death, without being the "life of the spirit," but still death, the other of death which is itself only the other, infinite alteration, we other mortals, our existences on the threshold.

To this there is no access, no entry. This is where we entered, coming from afar, from very near, touching with our bare feet the copper basin and the woman's dress, not touching, touched.

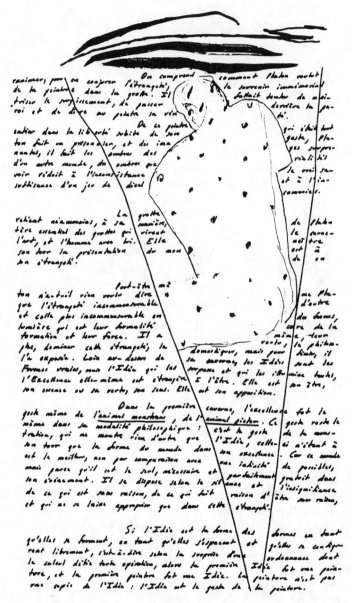

"Painting in the Grotto." Page reproduced from *La Part de l'oeil*, 10 (1994).

§ 4 Painting in the Grotto

Man began with the strangeness of his own humanity. Or with the humanity of his own strangeness. Through this strangeness he presented himself: he presented it, or figured it to himself. Such was the self-knowledge of man, that his presence was that of a stranger, monstrously similar [*semblable*]. The similar came before the self, and this is what it, the self, was. Such was his first knowledge, his skill, the quickness of the hand whose secret he wrested from the very strangeness of his nature, although he did not thereby penetrate a secret, but was penetrated by it, and himself exposed as the secret. The schema of man is the monstration of this marvel: self outside of self, the outside standing for *self*, and he being surprised in face of self. Painting paints this surprise. This surprise is painting.

Everything is given at one blow in this monstration: the society of fellow men [*des semblables*], the troubling familiarity of animals, the subject looming up from its death, the suspended sense, the obscure obviousness. Everything is given in this quick turn of the hand that traces the contours of a strange presence, right at a wall, a bark, or a skin (he could have crushed it or smothered it there almost with the same gesture). It was perhaps, also, a chant. One must hear the first singer accompanying the first painter.

The pleasure men take in *mimēsis* is made up of the troubling feeling that comes over them in the face of recognizable strangeness, or in the excitement that comes from a recognition that one would have to say is *estranged*.

I recognize there that I am unrecognizable to myself, and without that there would be no recognition. I recognize that this makes for a being as well as a non-being, and that I am one in the other. I am the being-one-in-the-other. The same is the same without ever returning to itself, and this is how it identifies with itself. The same is the same of an identity that alters itself from birth, thirsting after a self that has never yet been self, and whose birth is already alteration, and who appropriates itself as this very alteration.

The traced figure presents all that. It is the trace of the strangeness that comes like an open intimacy, an experience more internal than any intimacy, deep-set like the grotto, open like the aperity and the appearance of its wall. The traced figure is this very opening, the spacing by which man is brought into the world, and by which the world itself is a world: the event of all presence in its absolute strangeness.

Thus, the painting that begins in the grottos (but also the grottos that painting invents) is first of all the monstration of the commencement of being, before being the beginning of painting.

Man began with the knowledge of this monstration. *Homo sapiens* is only what it is by virtue of *Homo monstrans*.

In a single blow, in a same first gesture, about twenty-five thousand years ago, the *animal monstrans* shows itself. It would show nothing if it did not show itself showing. It shows in a stroke the stranger that it is, it shows the strangeness of the world to the world, and it also shows its knowledge of monstration and of its estrangement. For "to show" [*montrer*] is nothing other than to set aside, to set at a distance of presentation, to exit from pure presence, to make absent and thus to absolutize.

What men subsequently will name with a word that means knowledge and know-how, *tekhnē* or *ars*, is at man's beginning the total of his science and his consciousness. (But will he ever have ceased beginning again?) Science and consciousness of fascination with the monster of presence exited from presence. *Tekhnē* or *ars* of a fascination that does not paralyze, but that turns the light or serious abandon over to non-knowledge. This fascination does not fix on the image, except to let bottomless appearance—aperity, resemblance without original, or yet again, the origin itself as monster and endless monstration—come forward. Art's quick turn of the hand is the turning of this gesture.

In this sense, "art" is there in its entirety from the beginning. It consists in that: being there in its entirety at the beginning. "Art" is the beginning itself, and it traverses, like a single, immobile gesture, the twenty-five thousand years of the *animal monstrans*, of the *animal monstrum*. But at the same time it continually transforms the forms of this infinite monstration. With a single stroke, it multiplies endlessly the history of all its strokes. Art is but an immense tradition of the invention of the arts, of the birth of endless forms of knowledge. For what is properly monstrous, the monstrosity of the proper, is that there is no end to the finiteness of the figure.

The sense that is the world right at or right next to itself, this immanent sense of being *there* and nothing else, comes to show its transcendence there, which is to have no sense, to neither engage nor permit its own assumption into any kind of Idea or End, but to present itself always as its own estrangement. (To be *there* inasmuch as the *there* is *there*, monstrously there, is to be *the there* itself, to incise or excise the intimate with its immanence, to carve or paint the wall, its appar(t)ition: the *there* is always a grotto.)

If the condition of a presence, in general, is its situation in a place, in a time, and for a subject, then the world, and man in the world, is the presentation of a presence without presence. For the world has neither time, nor place, nor subject. It is pure and simple monstrous presentation, which shows itself as such in the gesture of the man tracing the contours of the apparition that nothing either supports or delimits.

～

Thus, the traced hands, probably with the help of some stenciling technique (what are called "negative hands"), which are today the earliest known paintings (Cosquer Cave, and elsewhere hundreds of hands that are a little more recent), next to animals and various signs, these hands present nothing other than presentation itself, its open gesture, its displaying, its aperity, its patefaction— and its stupefaction. The hand posed, pressed against the wall, grasps nothing. It is no longer a prehensile hand, but is offered like the form of an impossible or abandoned grasp. A grasp that could as well let go. The grasp of a letting go: the letting go of form.

Detached from any taking and from any undertaking other than that of exposing itself, in a chiromancy with nothing to decipher, the hand of the first painter, the first self-portrait, shows itself naked and silent, assuming an insignificance that is altogether denied when it grasps an instrument, an object, or prey.

These grottos show no trace of habitation nor even, or only very little, of use. From this, it is thought one can deduce that they were "sanctuaries." But it would be rash to associate this fact necessarily with the representation of a cult and of the exalted or fearful encounter with a divinity, with a *numen* in relation to which the painted images would have performed a propitiatory or evocative function. There is in fact no reason to lend these forms and figures any other sense than the sense without signification of the exposi- tion whereby presence makes itself a stranger, holding the world and the subject up before themselves as before an absent sense: not a lost sense, nor one that is distanced or deferred, but a sense given in the absence as in the most simple estranged simplicity of pres- ence—*being* without being or without essence that founds it, causes it, justifies it, or sanctifies it. Being simply existing. Being even sovereignly existing, for it is governed by nothing but this existence itself.

And showing, there, its sovereignty.

But this sovereignty is not exercised over anything; it is not domination. It is not exercised; in truth, it is exceeded: its whole exercise is to exceed itself, not being itself anything but the absolute detachment or distancing of what has no foundation in the prop- erty of a presence, immanent or transcendent, and of what is thus in itself the lack, the failing of a presence that shows itself as a stranger to self, in itself a stranger to self, sovereignly alienated. Its exposed failing is its own proper touch, its honor, its grace, and its harmony, at the most intimate point of the rending and the mute stridency that traverses it—harmony and rhythm of the form, music right at the surface of the painting.

Image, here, is not the convenient or inconvenient double of a thing in the world: it is the glory of that thing, its epiphany, its distinction from its own mass and its own appearance. The image praises the thing as detached from the universe of things and shown to be detached as is the whole of the world. (The whole of the world is detached from self: it is detachment.)

~

The silence of the first paintings is not that of an era whose voices would have become extinct for us. It is not even clear that we do not hear, along with these paintings, the chants of those men (heard as that which is touched by the eye, heard in their absolute proximity to and distance from the visible form). But it is then the silence of all painting, of all music, the silence of the form, of this form that neither signifies nor flatters but that shows: the rhythm or the schema, the line or the cadence. Neither is it therefore the silence that holds back and keeps in reserve, but the silence that lets the strangeness of being occur: its immediate contiguity, right at the wall. The silence does nothing: it exposes everything.

This silence neither precedes speech nor succeeds it: it is the tension of speech, the vibration that lets no meaning weigh down or weigh in. Silence of a humanity without set speeches (but not without speech), which has no relation to its ends, which nothing causes to be taken as anything other than what it is: the simple strangeness of presentation. (A humanity without humanism.)

Do we imagine (and according to what image, what idea of the "image"?) this, as one says, "primitive" humanity, this "stammering," "crude" humanity, in the process of giving itself shape, all at once at the same time and with the same gesture entirely thrown into its very sketch, as this sketch, at one stroke right away finished (the sketch as the culmination), whose sketches will have been taken up again continuously by twenty-five thousand years of painting, without all the same closing off the form (the culmination as sketch)?

Everything about this properly inhuman and thus monstrous strangeness is very simple, sober, and even strict, without fuss and without ornament other than the apparel of appearance. The silence of the first paintings does not come, therefore, from the extinction of the chants or the sacred acclamations that would have accompanied them and offered commentary on them. To the contrary, this silence was the unheard-of chant that nothing caused to submit to any service, either divine or profane.

Man began in the calmly violent silence of a gesture: here, on the wall, the continuity of being was interrupted by the birth of a form, and this form, detached from everything, even detaching the wall from its opaque thickness, gave one to see the strangeness of the being, substance, or animal that traced it, and the strangeness of all being in him.

At this, man trembled, and this trembling was him.

If we are moved, fascinated, and touched in our souls by the images from the caves of our prehistory (which is so little ours even as it is ours, which is our defamiliarization within our own family), it is not only because of their troubling antiquity, but rather because we sense the emotion that was born with them, this emotion that was their very birth (*or whose coming into the world they were?*): laughter and fear, desire and astonishment in the face of this obviousness, as powerful as the wall of massive rock, according to which the figural contour completes what cannot be completed, finishes the non-finite, and does not thereby withdraw it from the infinite but, quite the contrary, gives it the dizzying space of its presentation without end.

Beneath the earth, as if touching on the rupture of any support and on the foundation of any distance, the whole world surfaced . . .

. . . one more time: what was then this additional "time," this second occurrence or this recurrence of the origin, this re-creation that recreated the creator himself?

～

Let us imagine the unimaginable, the gesture of the first imager. He proceeds neither at random nor according to a project. His hand advances into a void, hollowed out at that very instant, which separates him from himself instead of prolonging his being in his act. But this separation is the act of his being. Here he is outside of self even before having been his own self, before having been a self. In truth, this hand that advances opens by itself this void, which it does not fill. It opens the gaping hole of a presence that has just absented itself by advancing its hand.

The latter gropes along, blind and deaf to any form. For the animal that stands in the grotto and that makes this gesture knows things, beings, different kinds of matter, structures, signs, and actions. But it is ignorant of form, the rising up of a figure or a rhythm in its presentation. He is ignorant of it, or he is immediately that very thing: the arising of form, figuration.

For the first time, he touches the wall not as a support, nor as an obstacle or something to lean on, but as a place, if one can touch a place. Only as a place in which to let something of interrupted being, of its estrangement, come about. The rock wall makes itself merely spacious: the event of dimension and of the line, of the setting aside and isolation of a zone that is neither a territory of life nor a region of the universe, but a spacing in which to let come— coming from nowhere and turned toward nowhere—all the presence of the world.

From the painter to the wall, the hand opens a distance that suspends the continuity and the cohesion of the universe, in order to open up a world. The surface of stone becomes this suspension itself, its relief, its nuance, and its grain. The world is as if cut, cut off from itself, and it assumes a figure on its cutaway section: flattened, freed from inert thickness, form without ground, abyss and shore of apparition.

The line divides and sets out the form: it forms the form. It separates at the same moment—with the same deftness, with the same drafted line—the tracing animal and his gesture: at the point of the flint or the finger springs forth the separated real, the real suddenly drawn or destined according to its pure and simple reality, offered as such on a slope of wall, without substance, without weight, without resistance to its outspread display. The very reality of the real, detached from any use, impracticable, untreatable, even untouchable, dense and porous, opaque and diaphanous right at the wall, an impalpable and impassive film on the surface of the rock: the rock itself is transfigured, surfaced, but still solid.

Not a presence, but its vestige or its birth, its nascent vestige, its trace, its monster.

~

At the advancing tip of the first tracing, the first painter sees coming toward him a monster who holds out to him the unsuspected reverse side of presence, its displacement, its detachment, or its folding into pure manifestation, and the manifestation itself as the coming of the stranger, as the birth into the world of what has no place in the world, as the birth of the origin itself, or as the appearance of appearing, the enlargement of being in its existence (as one says or used to say: to set a prisoner *at large*).

But what has no place *in* the world is the coming of the world, its event. In a sense, it is nothing other than the world itself, or its pure act: it is the fact *that there is* world. This remains forever a stranger in the world, nowhere taken up in the world, in no place, but at the same time it is spread everywhere over the surface of the world as the most immediate taking-place of this world, its "continued creation": an immediacy such that it right away spurts outside of itself, completely turned inside out into the exterior manifestation of forms.

The world, moreover, is but surfaces on surfaces: however far one penetrates behind the wall, there are only other walls, other slices, and strata beneath strata or faces on faces, indefinite foliation of layers of the obvious. By painting the wall, the *animal monstrans* does not set a figure on a support; rather, he takes away the thickness of this support, he multiplies it indefinitely, and it is itself no longer supported by anything. There is no more ground, or else the ground is but the coming about of forms, the appearance of the world.

(The interdiction on representation is the interdiction on reproducing the divine gesture of creation. But here, there is nothing of the kind to reproduce, and therefore no interdiction. It is man who remains interdicted, dumbfounded before the looming up of his strangeness. He experiences the absolute necessity of rediscovering this looming up. He must reproduce the apparition, it is imperative: imitation is an intimation. All the same, one must not forget that the strangeness looms up only in this gesture of imitation. *Mimēsis*, monstrosity, monstration turn in a circle.)

This is the event that manifests itself at the point of the painter's flint or charcoal in the grotto: here he is who knows he is miming the origin of the world. He does not copy this origin; he plays at the posture that has never taken place and that will never take place, since there is no outside the world. (There is only the inside of the world, like the inside of a grotto.) He plays at the posture or the attitude of the gesture that gives rise and gives place to the world (that gives it place without having any prior place of its own). The grotto is the world, where the drawing causes the impossible outside of the world to loom up, and causes it to loom up in its very impossibility.

Captured in this posture, in the middle of this gesture, the first painter sees himself, and the world along with him, come toward self like the one he never was and never will be, like the stranger come from nowhere and going nowhere, therefore neither coming nor going, but simply posed, detached, isolated by a line in front of self. Self, he surprises himself absent just as the author of the world is absent. He thus surprises the world in its nudity of being or of a being without author. He is amazed, he is worried, and he is brought to laughter by this posture and by what it shows him: the form of the animal, his own form, and that of being itself, cut out in front of him, left like a trace that leads to nothing but the wall of the grotto and to the superb images.

∼

One can understand why Plato wanted to revive, so as to conjure away its strangeness, the immemorial memory of the painting in the grotto. It was necessary to try to master the looming up, to go behind the wall and tell the painter the truth.

Out of this painter wrapped up in the sudden freedom of his gesture, Plato makes a prisoner; out of the surprising images, he makes shadows of the realities of another world, shadows that true knowledge reduces to the inconsistency and insufficiency of a play of cutout figures.

Plato's grotto, nevertheless, retains in its own way the essential character of the grottos that witnessed the birth of art, and of man with it. In its turn this grotto is the presentation of the world in its strangeness.

It may even be that Plato meant to say nothing other than the incommensurable strangeness of forms, and the even more incommensurable strangeness of light, which is their very formality, their formation, and their force. He, the philosopher, wanted to dominate this strangeness, domesticate it, but in the end he exposed it. Far above his cave, Ideas are the true Forms, but the Idea that surpasses them and illuminates them all, Excellence, is a stranger to being. It is the being of being, its essence or its virtue: its sense. It is being's apparition.

In the first cave, excellence was the very gesture of the *animal monstrans*, the *animal pictor*. This gesture remains the same in its philosophical modality: it is the gesture of monstration, which shows nothing other than the Idea, the Idea being in its turn but the form of the world in its excellence. For this world is the best one, not through comparison with an infinity of possible worlds, but because it is the only one, necessary and perfectly gratuitous in its event. It sets itself out according to the silence and insignificance of that which is without reason, of that which makes a reason of being without reason, and which does not let itself be appropriated except in this strangeness.

If the Idea is the form of forms inasmuch as they take form, inasmuch as they space themselves out and configure themselves freely, that is, according to the surprise of an ordering whose calculation defies all operation, then the first Idea was a painting and the first painting was an Idea. Painting is not a copy of the Idea: the Idea is the gesture of painting.

~

The images refer us back to the image of the painter, the brilliant flash of his gesture drawn taut by the Idea, the gesture that is already the Idea before the latter idealizes itself: the monster that is neither beautiful, nor ugly, nor true, nor false, but that merely comes forward right here, sprung up from no other place.

The stretched-out hand follows the traced line that decides in advance of the hand and pulls it along the wall of the grotto. In one sense, it is a pure touching of the rock, of its resistance, and of its docility to the incision and the mark, of the constraints created by its contours, of its density. In another sense, it is touch divided against itself, separating the hand from the stone, opening continuity into distinct places and contrasted values, figuring the figure that suddenly offers up its unpolished brilliance.

There is more than one tracing of the trace: there is the engraving of the flint, the imprint of crushed charcoal, the paste or powder made from soil, there are lines and colors, glues and acids. There are also the chants we no longer hear, and the steps of the dance we no longer see. Each time, the gesture differs and the trace is never one, but always distinct from another, always taking shape in a singular grain or tone, in a thickness or in a moiré that are each time the unique properties of the monster, of a different monster. It shows nothing other than its manner—its *tekhnē mimētikē*—of showing itself, of configuring its absence of figure. It never resembles itself, being the monster and the monstrator [*montre*] of resemblance that itself resembles nothing, thereby miming the excellent nature of the world, the world or man, being or the stranger.

So the eye, which up until then had done nothing but perceive things, discovers itself seeing. It sees this: that it sees. It sees that it sees *there*: it sees there where there is something of the world that shows itself. And this is always also to see there in the night of the grotto, the gaze stretched straight ahead into the black depths. And the gaze sees there the Idea, the (feminine) stranger, the figure: it is opened by and in this figure, its rhythm is set by "her," and it is "she," the Monster that it is itself. The Monster sees the invisible, and the vanishing sense of its own presence in the world.

§ 5 The Vestige of Art

What remains of art? Perhaps only a vestige. That at least is what we are hearing today, once again. By proposing "The Vestige of Art" as a title for this essay, I have in mind first of all, quite simply, this: on the assumption that there remains in fact only a vestige of art—both an evanescent trace and an almost ungraspable fragment—that itself could be just the thing to put us on the track of art itself, or at least of something that would be essential to it, if one can entertain the hypothesis that what *remains* is also what *resists* the most. As a next step we will wonder if this something essential might not itself be of the order of a vestige, and if art in its entirety does not best manifest its nature, or what is at stake in it, when it becomes a vestige of itself, when, that is, having retreated from the greatness of works that cause worlds to come into being, art seems past, showing nothing more than its passage. We will come to this in a moment, when we consider in detail what a vestige is.

Thus, there is a debate around contemporary art, and it is by virtue of this debate that you have asked me to speak today, in the Jeu de Paume, in a museum—that is, in this strange place where art *only passes*: it remains there as passed/past, and it is just *passing through* there, among the sites of life and presence that perhaps, doubtless most often, it will never again rejoin. (But perhaps the museum is "not a place, but a history," as Jean-Louis Déotte has put it,[1] an ordering that gives rise to the passage as such, to the *passing* rather than to the *past*—which is the business of the vestige.)

People everywhere are wondering, anxiously, aggressively, if art today is still art. A promising situation, contrary to what disgruntled minds believe, since it proves that people are concerned with what art *is*. In other words, and in a very heavy word, with its *essence*. The word is, in fact, weighty, and no doubt it will cause some to form suspicions about the philosophical seizure or capture it might announce. But we will do our best to pare down the weight of this word, right down to its own vestige. For the moment, let us respond to what is promising there. Does this debate allow us to know a little bit more about the "essence" of art?

To begin with, one must clarify things, because there are several debates, which intertwine. Doubtless they have a common ground or vanishing point in the *being* of art, but one must distinguish several levels. I am going to advance progressively, distributing my remarks in simple successive numbers (exactly ten).

~

1. First of all, there would be the debate concerning the art market, or concerning art as market—as reducing itself to a market, which would be a first manner of emptying out its proper being. It is a debate, as we know, about the sites or the places, about the instances or the functions of this market, about the public and private institutions that are mixed up in it, about the place it takes up in a "culture" that, on a larger scale, is already in itself a bone of contention.

I will not fully pursue all of this here, because I am not competent to do so. I propose merely a reflection on the essence of art, or on its vestige—and thus on the history that leads to this vestige. This does not immediately yield principles from which one could deduce practical maxims. The negotiation between the two registers is of another sort. I am therefore not proposing a "theory" for a "practice"—neither a practice of the market nor, and if possible even less, an artistic practice.

But since I have come up against the motif of the relation of art to the discourses put forward about it, and since, in recent years, some have understood certain of these discourses as indicative of a philosophical inflation and as participating, in a more or less underhanded way, in the extortion of a surplus value on, or behind the back of art, I seize the opportunity to affirm, on the contrary, that the work of thinking and speaking art, or its vestige, is itself, in a singular manner, taken or woven into the working of art itself. This has been so ever since there has been "art" (regardless of when one chooses to date its birth, with Lascaux or with the Greeks, or with the detachment, the *distinction*, in effect, that is called "end of art"). In each of its gestures, art also sets in motion the question of its "being": it quests after its own trace. Perhaps it always has with itself a relation of vestige—and of investigation.

(Reciprocally, many works of art today, far too many, perhaps, are finally nothing but their own theory, or at least seem to be nothing but that—yet another form of vestige. But this is itself a symptom of the muffled exigency that is worrying artists and that is not at all "theoretical": the exigency of presenting "art" itself, the exigency of its own *ekphrasis*.)

All the same, I will add this about the market: stigmatizing the subordination of works to financial capitalism is not sufficient to account for what puts art in the position of exorbitant value—or for what makes it, so to speak, exorbit value itself (use value, exchange value, and moral value, as well as semantics).

It is not a matter of excusing, still less of legitimating, anything. It is not a matter of neglecting the fact that the market touches not only on the buying and selling of works, but on the works themselves. It is only a matter of saying: the score is not settled by a condemnation of aesthetic morals. This is nothing new in the history of art, which does not wait for us to come along in order to be a history of merchandizing, too. (What is new is but a state of the economy or of capital; in other words, the question is *political* in the most intense, abrupt, and difficult sense of the word.) No doubt art has always been *priceless*, by excess or by lack. This exorbitation has to do—across many mediations, deviations, and expropriations—with one of the most difficult, delicate stakes in the task of thinking art: to think, to weigh, to evaluate what is archi-precious or priceless, inestimable about it. In the manner of a vestige.

2. As for the debate that will be called "properly aesthetic," let us distinguish two levels.

First level: the incomprehension and the hostility aroused by contemporary art are matters of *taste*. Thus, all discussion is acceptable. Not by virtue of a subjectivist liberalism of tastes and colors (in which there is no *discussion*), but because taste (as long as one does not go to the other extreme and confuse it with the normative drive or maniacal discrimination), in the debate of tastes and distastes, is but the work of form as it seeks itself, of style that is still unaware of itself as it takes form, and that *senses* itself when it cannot yet recognize its *sense*. Taste, the debate about taste, is the promise or the proposition of art, symmetrical with its vestige. It is the proposition of a form, of a sketch for an age or for a world. For this reason, I would prefer that there be more debate than there is . . . That there be once again, in a different way, battles over *Hernani* or Dada . . . I will not go any further in this direction, which, as we know, comes from Kant (except to remark that if it is not possible, at this moment, to propose a "world," this supposed failing is not in any case to be imputed to art and to artists, as some people do, but rather to the "world" or to its absence . . .).

Second level (which does not exclude the first, but in which it is no longer a question of taste): the incomprehension and the hostility, no less than the frenzied approbation, themselves correspond, without knowing or without wanting to know, to the fact that art can no longer be understood or received according to the schemas that once belonged to it. Any use of the word "art" retains inevitably something of these schemas: when we say "art," the connotation is "great art," that is, something like the idea of a "great form" that would intentionally border on the cosmology of its time (to paraphrase Lawrence Durrell in *The Alexandria Quartet*). In saying "art," we evoke a cosmetics that has a *cosmic*, *cosmological,* even a *cosmogonic* import or stake. But if there is no *kosmos,* how can there be an art in this sense? And that there is no *kosmos* is doubtless the decisive mark of our world: *world,* today, does not mean *kosmos.* As a consequence, "art" cannot mean "art" in this sense. (That is why the first title I proposed for today's lecture was "Art Without Art.")

By inscribing the *polis* in the *kosmos,* we could also exemplify the preceding with this sentence from Georges Salles: "An art differs from the one that precedes it and realizes itself because it sets forth a reality of a nature different from a simple plastic modification: it reflects another man. . . . The moment one must seize is the one in which a plastic plenitude responds to the birth of a social type."[2] But just as our world is no longer *cosmic,* our *polis* is perhaps no longer *political* in the sense suggested by these lines.

To the determination of this acosmic world and this "apolitical" city, one must not forget to add this, which plays more than a minor role and is summed up by the well-known sentence from Adorno: "All post-Auschwitz culture, including its urgent critique, is garbage."[3] Besides its value as a name, "Auschwitz" has here the function of a metonymy for so many other instances of the unbearable. This sentence, nonetheless, does not justify the conversion of garbage into works of art. On the contrary, it gives back a terrible echo—for example, of a remark made in 1929, well before the war, by Michel Leiris: "At present, there is no longer any way to make something pass for ugly or repulsive. Even shit is pretty."[4] The intrication of world and filth [*du monde et de l'immonde*] cannot be, for us, either disintricated or dissimulated. It is thus that there is no *kosmos.* But we have no concept for an art without *kosmos* or *polis,* if there must at least be an art of this sort, or if it must still be a question of "art."

Thus, all the accusations, all the attributions, exhortations, and convocations addressed to art from the supposed horizon of a *kosmos* and a *polis* to which there would be reason to respond or to intentionally border on, all of these are in vain because this supposition is, for us, not supported by anything. For this reason, it is not possible to suppose a region or a domain of "art" to which one could address oneself, to which one could address demands, orders, or prayers.

To this extent—an immense extent, in truth, incommensurable—art in our time imposes on itself a severe gesture, a painful move toward its own essence become enigma, a manifest enigma of its own vestige. This is not the first time: perhaps the whole history of art is made up of tensions and torsions toward its own enigma. The tension and the torsion seem to have reached their high point today. This is perhaps but an appearance; perhaps it is as well the concentration of an event that began at least two centuries ago—or since the beginnings of the West. Whatever the case may be, "art" vacillates in its meaning as much as "world" does in its order or in its destination. In this regard, all quarrels are pointless: we *must* accompany this movement, we must *know* how to do it. This is of the order of the strictest duty and knowledge, and not of the order of blind fits of anger, execrations, or celebrations.

3. It is worth recalling that the fits of anger, the signs of distress, and the certifications of exhaustion are themselves already quite used up. Kant wrote that "a boundary is set to [art] beyond which it cannot go, which presumably has been reached long ago and cannot be extended further."[5] This boundary is opposed, in the Kantian context, to the indefinite growth of knowledge; this is not exactly a certification of exhaustion, but it is the first form of a certification of "end," through the ambiguous motif of a *finishing* of art that is always begun again. Hegel, as is only too well known, declared that art, as manifestation of the true, belonged to the past. At the other end of the century, Renan, in what was no doubt a deliberate replay of Hegel, wrote: "Even great art will disappear. The time will come when art will be a thing of the past." Duchamp stated: "Art has been thought through to the end."[6]

A commentary on merely these four sentences, and on their succession, would require an enormous study. I will anticipate here merely its conclusion: art has a history, it is perhaps history in a radical sense, that is, not progress but passage, succession, appearance, disappearance, event.[7] But *each time* it offers *perfection*, completion. Not perfection as final goal and term toward which one advances, but the perfection that has to do with the coming and the presentation of a single thing inasmuch as it is formed, inasmuch as it is completely conformed to its being, in its *entelechy*, to use a term from Aristotle that means "a being completed in its end, perfect." Thus it is a perfection that is always *in progress*, but which admits no progression from one entelechy to another.

Therefore, the history of art is a history that withdraws at the outset and always from the history or the historicity that is represented as process or as "progress." One could say: art is each time radically *another art* (not only another form, another style, but another "essence" of "art"), according to its "response" to another world, to another *polis*; but it is at the same time each time *all* that it is, *all art* such as in itself finally . . . [8]

But this completion without end—or rather, this *finite finishing*, if one attempts to understand thereby a completion that limits itself to what it is, but that, to achieve that very thing, opens the possibility of another completion, and that is therefore also *infinite finishing*—this paradoxical mode of per-fection is doubtless what our whole tradition demands one to think and avoids thinking *at the same time*. There are profound reasons, which we will touch on later, for this ambiguous gesture. Thus, this tradition designates as a boundary, as an *end* in the banal sense, and very quickly as a *death*, what might well be in truth the suspension of a form, the instantaneousness of a gesture, the blackout [*syncope*] of an appearance—and thus also, each time, of a disappearance. Are we capable of thinking this? Which is to say, you guessed it, of thinking the vestige?

It will have to be done. For if the event of art completing itself and vanishing is repeated throughout its history, if such an event forms this history as the rhythm of its repetition (and this, I repeat, perhaps in silence ever since Lascaux), it is because some necessity attaches to it. We will not escape from it by way of exorcisms or benedictions. Consequently, just as I am not seeking here a judgment of taste, neither am I proposing a *final* judgment on contemporary art, a judgment that would measure it, for good or for ill, against the ruler of teleological finishing (which would also be, necessarily, theological and thus anthropological and cosmological). I propose, on the contrary, to examine the kind of "perfection" or "finite/infinite finishing" that is possible from what *remains* once a completion exhibits itself and insists on exhibiting itself. My concern, then, is this: with a *finite or vestigial per-fection*.

4. If we pay attention and weigh words and their history carefully, we will agree that there is a definition of art that encompasses all the others (for the West at least, but art is a Western concept). It is, not at all by chance, Hegel's definition: art is *the sensible presentation of the Idea*. No other definition escapes from this one sufficiently to oppose it in any fundamental way. It encloses, up until today, the being or essence of art. If one allows for several versions or nuances, it is valid from Plato to Heidegger (at least to the best-known version of *The Origin of the Work of Art*; things are different in the first version of this text, as published by Emmanuel Martineau in 1987, but I cannot here get into the necessary analysis). Beyond this, there is us: we struggle with each other and we debate over an inside/outside of this definition; to us falls the responsibility of debating with it, with this inevitable and yet already exceeded definition, as I would like to show.

Not only does this definition haunt philosophy, but it commands definitions that would seem to be distant from philosophical discourse. To take a few examples, the formula by Durrell says nothing else; nor does this one, from Joseph Conrad: "Art itself may be defined as a single-minded attempt to render the highest kind of justice to the visible universe, by bringing to light the truth, manifold and one, underlying its every aspect";[9] nor this other one, whose proximity is merely better disguised, which is taken from Martin Johnson and proposed to Norman Mailer in an interview: "Art is the communication of emotion";[10] nor this one, from Dubuffet: "No art without intoxication. But this means: mad intoxication! let reason be overthrown! delirium! Art is the most enthralling orgy within man's reach."[11]

In order to grasp not the simple identity but the profound homogeneity of these formulae, it suffices to recall that the Hegelian Idea is not at all the intellectual Idea. It is neither the ideat (or product) of a notion, nor the ideal of a projection. Rather, the Idea is the gathering in itself and for itself of the determinations of being (to go quickly, we can also call it truth, sense, subject, being itself). The Idea is the presentation to itself of being or the thing. It is thus its internal conformation and its visibility, or in other words, it is the thing itself as vision/envisioned [*en tant que vue*], where, in French, the word *vue* is taken both as noun (the thing as a visible form) and as adjective (the thing *seen, envisioned,* grasped in its form, but from within itself or its essence).

In this regard, art is the sensible visibility of this intelligible, that is, invisible, visibility. The invisible form—Plato's *eidos*—returns to itself and appropriates itself as visible. Thus, it brings into the light of day and manifests the being of its Form and its form of Being. All the great theories of "imitation" have never been anything but theories of the imitation, or the image, of the Idea (which is itself, you understand, but the *self-imitation* of being, its transcendent or transcendental miming)—and reciprocally, all thinking about the Idea is thinking about the image or imitation. Including, and especially, when it detaches itself from the imitation of external forms or from "nature" understood in this way. All this thinking is thus theological, turning obstinately around the great motif of *"the visible image of the invisible God,"* which for Origen is the definition of Christ.

Therefore, all of modernity that speaks of the invisible or the unpresentable is always at least on the verge of renewing this motif. It is the motif that, to give another example, directs the words of Klee engraved on his tomb, and quoted by Merleau-Ponty: *"I cannot be caught in immanence."*[12]

What matters, then, is this: a visibility of invisibility as such, or ideality made present, even if it be the paradoxical presence of its abyss, its darkness, or its absence. This is what makes for the *beautiful,* ever since Plato and even more, perhaps, since Plotinus, for whom, in the access to beauty, it is a question of becoming oneself pure light and vision, in beauty's intimacy, and thus becoming "the only eye capable of seeing supreme beauty."[13] Supreme beauty, or the brilliant flash of truth, or the sense of being. Art, or the sensible sense of absolute sense. And once again this is what makes for a beautiful that goes beyond itself into the "sublime," then into the "terrible," as well as into the "grotesque," into the implosion of "irony," in a general entropy of forms or into the pure and simple position of a ready-made object.

5. Some, perhaps, will hasten to conclude: here indeed is the reason art is in perdition, because there is no longer any Idea to present, or because the artist no longer wants to do so (or else has lost the sense of the Idea). There is no more sense, or else we no longer want any; we are stuck in the refusal of sense and in the will to an end with which Nietzsche characterizes nihilism. So we ask the artist, more or less explicitly, to rediscover the Idea, the Good, the True, the Beautiful . . .

Such is the discourse, as weak here as it is elsewhere, of those who believe that it suffices to wave the flag of "values" and to fling about moral exhortations. Even if one must admit that there is some nihilism in this or that artist (in the one who, as Nietzsche puts it, "advances cynical history, cynical nature"),[14] one will still have to analyze in an altogether different way where it comes from, and consequently also draw other consequences from it. To the extent to which art touches on an extremity, to the extent to which it attains a moment of completion and/or of suspension, but remains at the same time under the definition and under the prescription of "the sensible presentation of the Idea," it comes to a stop and freezes as if on the last brilliant sliver [*éclat*] of the Idea, on its pure and somber residue. At the limit, ultimately, there remains nothing more than the Idea of art itself, like a pure gesture of presentation folded back on itself. But this residue still functions as Idea, and even as pure Idea of pure sense, or like an ideal visibility without any other content than light itself: like the pure kernel of darkness in an absolute self-imitation.

Nothing is more Platonic, or more Hegelian, than certain forms in which a purity or a purification prevails, whether it be material, conceptual, minimalist, performative, or in the form of an event. One could say that this is the art of the residual Idea. Although it is residual, it unleashes no less, indeed more, an infinite desire for sense, and for the presentation of sense. This residual is not the vestigial that I will speak of. It is the reverse.

In truth, the remarkable feature of many works today is not found in the lack of form or in deformity, in the disgusting or in the anything-whatsoever: it is, rather, in the quest, the desire, or the will for sense. People want to *signify*—world and filth, technics and silence, subject and its absence, body, spectacle, insignificance, and pure will-to-signify. A "quest for sense" is the (more or less conscious) *leitmotiv* of those who forget, like the Wagner of *Parsifal*, that the structure of the quest is a structure of flight and loss, where the desired sense little by little sheds all its blood.

Thus the demand or the postulation of the Idea lets itself be grasped in its nakedness, in the flesh. All the more naked and laid bare in that these demands and postulations are the more deprived of both referents and the codes for those referents (which in the past were religion, myth, history, heroism, nature, feeling, before becoming those of vision or sensation itself, of texture and of matter, right up to self-referential form). Where this demand for the Idea is displayed, with fierceness and with naïveté, art exhausts and consumes itself: all that remains is its metaphysical desire. It is no longer anything but the gaping hole stretched toward its *end*, toward an empty *telos/theos* of which it still presents the image. A nihilism, therefore, but as the simple reversal of idealism. If for Hegel art is finite because the Idea comes round to presenting itself in its proper element, in the philosophical concept, for the nihilist art finishes itself by presenting itself in its proper—and empty— concept.

6. With this, however, we have not exhausted the resources of the definition of art—nor the resources of art itself. We are not yet at the end of its *end*. The end of art conceals yet one more supplementary complication, from which arises all the complexity of the

stakes of art today. To catch sight of it, we must take one more step in the logic of the "presentation of the Idea."

This step occurs in two moments, the first of which still belongs to Hegel (and through him to the whole tradition), whereas the second touches on Hegel's limit—and passes on to us (via Heidegger, Benjamin, Bataille, Adorno).

The first moment amounts to affirming that the "sensible representation of the Idea" is itself an absolute necessity of the Idea. In other words, the Idea cannot be what it is—presentation of the thing in its truth—except through, in, and as this sensible order that is at the same time its outside, and what is more, that is the outside as that which is withdrawn from the return-in-itself and for-itself of the Idea. The Idea must go outside itself in order to be itself. This is called the dialectical necessity. As you see, its implication is equivocal. On the one hand, art is therefore always necessary, and how could it end? But on the other hand, in the end it is the Idea that is presented. I will not linger any longer on this equivocation, although there is much to learn from the very specific manner in which it is at work in Hegel's *Aesthetics* and secretly complicates there, or even subverts, the schema of the "end of art."

But I move on to the second moment—the one that Hegel does not reach, cannot reach, and that remains as the residue of the equivocation (and therefore as that onto which this equivocation also opens, in its way). Succinctly put, this second moment can be stated as follows: the Idea, in presenting itself, withdraws as Idea. This statement must be carefully examined.

The presentation of the Idea is not the putting of what was inside on view on the outside, if the inside is what it is—"*inside*"—only outside and as outside. (At bottom, this is the strict logic of self-imitation.) Therefore, instead of finding itself again and returning to itself as the invisible ideality of the visible, the Idea effaces its ideality so as to be what it is—but what it "is," by the same token, it is not and can no longer be.

In other words: perhaps what *remains* to us of the philosophy of the Idea, that is, what remains to us to *think*, is that sense is its own withdrawal. But that the withdrawal of sense *is not once again an*

unpresentable Idea to be presented; this is what makes of this remainder, and of its thinking, indissociably a task for art: for if this
withdrawal is not an invisible ideality to be visualized, it is because
it is wholly tracing itself right at the visible, as the visible itself (or as
the sensible in general). A task for an art, consequently, that would
no longer be an art of a presentation of the Idea, and that should be
defined otherwise.

7. It is here that the remainder is vestige. If there is no invisible,
there is no visible image of the invisible. With the withdrawal of
the Idea, that is, with the event that shakes up the whole history of
the last two centuries (or the last twenty-five centuries . . .), the
image also withdraws. And as we shall see, the other of the image is
the vestige.

The image withdraws as phantom or phantasm of the Idea,
destined to vanish in ideal presence itself. It withdraws therefore as
image *of*, image of something or someone that, itself or himself or
herself, would not be an image. It effaces itself as simulacrum or as
face of being, as shroud or as glory of God, as imprint of a matrix or
as expression of something unimaginable. (Note in passing, because we will return to this, that it is perhaps first of all a very
precise image that gets effaced: man as the image of God.)

In this sense, far from being the "civilization of the image" that is
accused of crimes committed against art, we are rather a civilization
without image, because without Idea. Art, today, has the task of
answering to this world or of answering for it. It is not a matter of
making this absence of Idea into an image, for art then remains
caught in the ontotheological schema of the image of the invisible,
of the god that, as Montaigne said, one had to "imagine unimaginable." It is a question, then, of another task, whose givens we must
try to outline.

At the very least, it is clear that if art remains defined as a relation
of the image to the Idea, or of the image to the unimaginable (a
double relation that throughout the tradition determines more or
less the division between the beautiful and the sublime in the
philosophical determinations of art), then it is art as a whole that

withdraws along with the image. This is indeed what Hegel saw coming. If his formula has known such success, if it has been amplified and hijacked, it is quite simply because the formula was true and art was beginning to be done with its function as image. Which is to say, with its ontotheological function: it is indeed in religion or as religion that Hegelian art becomes a "thing of the past." But in this way it is perhaps art that was beginning or that was beginning again otherwise, beginning to become visible otherwise than as image, coming to make itself felt otherwise.

In a world without image in this sense, a profusion, a whirlwind of imageries unfolds in which one gets utterly lost, no longer finds *oneself* again, in which art no longer finds itself again. It is a proliferation of *views* [vues], the visible or the sensible itself in multiple brilliant slivers [*éclats*], which refer to nothing. Views that give nothing to be seen or that see nothing: views without *vision*. (Think of the effacement of the romantic figure in which the artist was *visionary*.) Or else, and in a symmetrical manner, this world is traversed by an "exacerbated" ban on images, as Adorno says, and thus "the ban itself has . . . come to evoke suspicions of superstition," suspicion that it is but anxiety before the "nothing" which would be the support of every image.[15] This "reference to nothing" thus opens onto a major ambiguity: either the "nothing," in an obstinate and I dare say obsessional manner, is still understood as negative of the Idea, as negative Idea, or as abyss of the Idea (as the void at the heart of its self-imitation)—or else it can be understood otherwise. This is what I would like to propose under the name of the *almost nothing* that is the vestige.

8. What remains withdrawn from the image, or what remains in its withdrawal, as that withdrawal itself, is the *vestige*. The concept of this word has been given to us initially, and doubtless not by chance, by theology and mysticism. We will proceed to take it from there, so as to appropriate it. Theologians put to work the difference between the image and the vestige in order to distinguish between the mark of God on the reasonable creature, on man *imago Dei*, and another mode of this mark on the rest of creation.

This other mode, the vestigial mode, is characterized as follows (I borrow the analysis of Thomas Aquinas): the vestige is an effect that "represents only the causality of the cause, but not its form."[16] Aquinas gives the example of smoke, of which fire is the cause. He adds, with reference to the sense of the word *vestigium*, which designates first of all the sole of a shoe or the sole of a foot, a trace, a footprint: "A vestige shows that someone has passed by but not who it is." The vestige does not identify its cause or its model, unlike the way (this is again Aquinas's example) "a statue of Mercury represents Mercury," which is an *image*. (One must also recall here that according to Aristotelian concepts the model is also a cause, the "formal" cause.)

In the statue, there is the Idea, the *eidos* and the idol of the god. In the vestigial smoke, there is no *eidos* of the fire. One could also say: the statue has an "inside," a "soul"; the smoke is without inside. Of the fire it keeps only its consumption. We say, "Where there's smoke, there's fire," but here smoke has value first of all as absence of fire, of the form of fire (unlike, Aquinas specifies, a fire lit as effect of lighting a fire). However, this absence is not considered as such; it is not to the unpresentability of the fire that one refers but to the presence of the vestige, to its remainder or to its clearing of a path of presence. (*Vestigium* itself comes from *vestigare*, "to follow on the traces," a word of unknown origin, one whose trace has been lost. It is not a "quest"; it is simply the act of putting one's steps in the traces of steps.)

Certainly, for theology, there is fire, the fire of God—and there is only fire that truly and fully is: the rest is cinders and smoke. (This is at least one pole of theological consideration, of which the other remains an affirmation and an approbation of all created things.) I am not seeking, then, a continuous derivation of "vestige" from theology, for in that case I would introduce what is still a remainder of theology. We have an example of how the vestige can be perfectly religious in the legendary margins of Islam: Mohammed's footprint at the moment of his departure into heaven. There is, moreover, behind Christian theology a whole biblical spirituality and theology of the trace and the passage. The point is, however, that the

trace of God remains *his* trace, and God is not effaced in it. We are
looking for something else: art indicates something else. Even over-
attention to this word "vestige," or to any other word, could harbor
a tendency to make of it a more or less sacred word, a kind of relic
(another form of the "remainder"). We have to handle here a
semantics that is itself vestigial: do not let the sense get set down
any more than the foot of a passerby.

In these conditions, what I am setting down here—which, I
believe, has been expressly proposed since Hegel—is that art is
smoke without fire, vestige without God, and not presentation of
the Idea. End of image-art, birth of vestige-art, or rather, coming
into the light of day of this: that art has always been vestige (and
that it has therefore always been removed from the ontotheological
principle). But how is one to understand that?

9. It would be necessary to distinguish, in art, between image
and vestige—right at the work of art and on the same work, on all
works perhaps. It would be necessary to distinguish that which
operates or demands an *identification* of the model or the cause,
even if it is a negative one, from that which proposes—or exposes—
merely the thing, *some thing*, and thus, in a sense, *anything whatsoever*, but not in any way whatsoever, not as the image of the
Nothing, and not as pure iconoclasm (which perhaps amounts to
the same thing). Some thing as vestige.

To attempt to discern the stakes of this singular concept, lodged
as a foreign body, difficult to spot, between presence and absence,
between everything and nothing, between image and Idea, in flight
from these dialectical couples, let us return to the *vestigium*. Recall
first of all that for the theologian the *vestigium Dei* is right at the
sensible, it is the sensible itself in its being-created. Man is *imago*
inasmuch as he is *rationalis*, but the *vestigium* is sensible. This is
also to say that the sensible is the element in which or as which the
image effaces and withdraws itself. The Idea gets lost there—
leaving its trace, no doubt, but not as the imprint of its form: as the
tracing, the step, of its disappearance. Not the form of its self-

imitation, nor the form in general of self-imitation, but what remains when self-imitation has not taken place.

Thus, if we do no more than take the step onto the limit of ontotheology, the step that succeeds Hegel, following Hegel but finally outside of him, the step into *the extremity of the end of art,* which ends that end in another event, then we are no longer dealing with the couple of the presenting sensible and the presented ideal. We are dealing with this: the form-idea withdraws and the vestigial form of this withdrawal is what our platonizing lexicon makes us call "sensible." *Aesthetics* as domain and as thinking of the sensible does not mean anything other than that. Here by contrast the trace is not the sensible trace of an insensible, one which would put us on its path or trail (which would indicate the way [*sens*] toward a Sense): it is (of) the sensible (the) *traced* or *tracing,* as its very *sense.* Atheism itself. This is doubtless what Hegel already understood.)

What can this mean? Let us try to advance further in our comprehension of the *vestigium.* This word designates the sole of the foot and its imprint or trace. From that one may draw two nonimagic traits. The foot, first of all, is the opposite of the face; it is the most dissimulated *face* or *surface* of the body. Here one might think of the presentation, which is finally atheological, of Mantegna's *Dead Christ,* the soles of the feet turned toward our eyes.[17] One may also recall that the word "face" comes from a root that means "to pose, to set": to pose, present, expose without reference to anything. Here, without relation to anything other than a ground that supports, but that is not a substratum or an intelligible *subject.* With the sole or the bottom of the foot [*la plante du pied*], we are in the domain of the flat, of the out-flat [*l'ordre du* plat *et de l'*à-plat], of horizontal extension without reference to vertical tension.[18]

Passage makes for the second trait: the vestige bears witness to a step, a walk, a dance, or a leap, to a succession, an élan, a repercussion, a coming-and-going, a *transire.* It is not a ruin, which is the eroded remains of a presence; it is just a touch right at the ground.

The vestige is the remains of a step, a *pas*.[19] It is not its image, for the step consists in nothing other than its own vestige. As soon as the *pas* is taken or made, it is past. Or rather, it is never, as step, simply "made" and set down somewhere. The vestige is its touch, or its operation, without being its work. Or in still other terms, those I was using a moment ago, it would be its *infinite finishing* (or *infinishing*) and not its *finite perfection*. There is no presence of the step, the *pas*; it is itself but coming to presence. It is impossible to say literally that the step takes *place*: yet a *place* in the strong sense of the word is always the vestige of a step. The step, which is its own vestige, is not an invisible—it is neither God nor the step of God— yet neither is it the simple slack surface of the visible. The step rhythms the visible with the invisible, or the other way around, if we must speak this language. This rhythm comprises sequence and syncopation, trajectory and interruption, gait and gap, phrase and spasm. It thereby cuts a *figure*, but this figure is not an image in the sense I have spoken of here.[20] The step of the figure, or the vestige, is its tracing, its spacing.

We must therefore renounce naming and assigning *being* to the vestige. The vestigial is not an essence—and no doubt this is what puts us on the track of the "essence of art." That art is today its own vestige, this is what opens us to it. It is not a degraded presentation of the Idea, nor the presentation of a degraded Idea; it presents what is not "Idea": motion, coming, passage, the going-on of coming-to-presence. Thus, in Dante's *Inferno*, an added settling of the boat or the sliding of a few stones indicate to the damned—but do not let them see—the invisible passage of a living soul.[21]

10. Having turned aside the question of being, we come upon that of the agent. It remains for us to ask: *whose* step is it? whose vestige?

It is not that of the gods, or at most it would be that of their departure. But this departure is as old as the art of Lascaux. If "Lascaux" does indeed signify "art," that is, if "art" did not arise progressively from under the layers of magic, and then religion, but indicates at the outset another posture, not the imprint of knees but the trace of the step, then the question of the image has never concerned art. Idolatry and iconoclasm have their place only in relation to the Idea. This in no way disputes the fact that art has been homogeneous to religions. (It would be necessary, moreover, to consider many differences among the latter.) But within religion itself, art is not religious. (Hegel would have understood this.)

Concerning the step of animals, there would be much to say: about their rhythms and their gaits, about their proliferated traces, vestiges of their paws or odors, and about that which in man is an animal vestige. Here again, one would have to turn in the direction of what Bataille called the "beast of Lascaux." (All of which presumes that one can overlook, on the other side of animality, all the other sorts of steps or passages, the pressures, frictions, contacts, all the touches, ridges, scratches, blotches, grazes . . .)

But I will take the risk of saying that the vestige is man's, of man. Not of the man-image, not of the man subject to the law of being the image of his own Idea, or of the Idea of his "own-ness" [*son propre*]. Thus of a man who fits the name "man" only with difficulty, if indeed it is difficult to remove that name from the Idea, from humanist theology. But let us say, let us try to say, no more than as an essay, *the passerby*. A passerby, each time, and each time *anyone whatsoever*—not that the passerby is anonymous, but his or her vestige does not identify him or her.[22] Each time then also *common*.

The passerby passes, *is* in the passage: what is also called *existing*. Existing: the passing being of being itself. Coming, departure, succession, passing the limits, moving away, rhythm, and syncopated blackout of being. Thus not the demand for sense, but the passage as the whole *taking place* of sense, as its whole presence. There would be two modes of being-present, the Idea and the being-before, preceding (not presenting), passing, and thus always-already passed/past. (In Latin, *vestigium temporis* was able to mean the very brief lapse of time, the moment or the instant: *Ex vestigio* = right away.)

The name of man, however, remains too much a name, an Idea, and an image—and it is not in vain that its effacement was announced. No doubt, to pronounce it again, in a completely other tone, is also to refuse the anguished prohibition on images without necessarily bringing back the man of humanism, that is, of self-imitation of the Idea. But, to finish and in passing, one might still try for an instant another word, by speaking of *gens*.[23] *Gens*, a vestige-word if there ever was one, name without name of the anonymous and the uncertain, a *generic* name par excellence, but one whose plural form would avoid generality, would indicate rather and on the contrary the singular insofar as it is always plural, and also the singular of *genres/genders*, of sexes, tribes (*gentes*), of peoples, of kinds [*genres*] of life, of forms (how many *genres* are there in art? how many genres of genres? but never any art that would have no genre . . .), and the singular/plural of *generations* and *engenderings*, that is, of successions and passages, of comings and departures, of leaps, of rhythms. *L'art et les gens*: I leave you with this title for another occasion.

Notes

Notes

Chapter 1

1. T. W. Adorno, *Aesthetic Theory*, trans. C. Lenhardt (London: Routledge & Kegan Paul, 1984), p. 260. Adorno is also the author of an essay, "Die Kunst und die Künste," from which we recall these sentences: "In relation to the arts, art is something that forms itself, contained potentially in each of them insofar as each must seek to liberate itself from the contingency of its quasi-natural moments by traversing them. But such an idea of art within the arts is not positive; it is nothing that one can grasp as simply present in them, but only as negation. . . . Art has its dialectical essence in that it accomplishes its movement toward unity only by passing through plurality. Otherwise the movement would be abstract and powerless. Its relation to the empirical order is essential to art itself. If it overlooks that relation, then what it takes to be its spirit remains exterior to it like any material whatsoever; it is only in the empirical order that the spirit becomes content. The constellation of art and the arts has its place within the concept of art" (in *Ohne Leitbild: Parva Aesthetica* [Frankfurt am Main: Suhrkamp Verlag, 1967], pp. 176–77). The contemporary question may well be that of the conceptual nonidentity of art, which gives rise to (or manifests itself as) the difficult-to-identify identity of "art in general," which revives in an entirely new manner the question of the particularity of the arts at the heart of this "generality," the latter effacing and at the same time reducing the former. Thus Thierry de Duve has written: "We should never cease to be amazed, or worried, by the fact that our age finds it perfectly legitimate that

someone be an artist without being a painter, or a writer, or a musician, or a filmmaker. . . . Has modernity invented *art in general?*" (*Au nom de l'art* [Paris: Editions de Minuit, 1989], back cover).

2. Adorno, *Aesthetic Theory*, p. 285. Elsewhere, Etienne Souriau has explicitly asked in *La Correspondance des arts*: "Whence comes the fact that there are several arts?" (Paris: Flammarion, 1969, pp. 67 and 101). But his response does not go beyond the diversity of what he calls the "sensible *qualia*" and the practical, technical, and social conditions of their operation. Any response that remains within the set of constraints which, in effect, cut up art from the outside does not touch upon the question. Recently, Gérard Granel has written: "There is no conceptual identity of Art, neither of the several arts taken together, nor of each one individually" ("Lecture de l'Origine," *L'Art au regard de la phénoménologie* [Toulouse: Presses Universitaires du Mirail, 1993], p. 94).

3. In Martin Heidegger, *Poetry, Language, Thought*, trans. Albert Hofstadter (New York: Harper and Row, 1971), p. 86. One would nevertheless have to specify that, by determining the essence of art in this fashion, Heidegger also leaves quite open, and even prescribed, the plurality of the arts as the only effectivity of such a remote "essence" (one which also comprehends, according to other passages, the necessity of the work as "thing." On this subject, see Alexander García Düttmann, *Das Gedächtnis des Denkens* [Frankfurt am Main: Suhrkamp, 1991], p. 220ff.). In another vein, one may also recall how the Nietzsche of *Richard Wagner in Bayreuth* could welcome the coming of the "total artistic genius" in an age when humanity had become accustomed to seeing the arts isolated from each other, as if that were the rule; see *Unfashionable Observations*, trans. Richard T. Gray (Stanford: Stanford University Press, 1995), pp. 261, 293.

4. We will translate *la technique* as "technics" when Nancy intends not technical skill, but the whole order of *tekhnē.*—Trans.

5. Plato, *The Symposium*, 205b. To gauge what is at stake in opening up the division between art and technics, one would need to recall a triple characteristic of *tekhnē*: it is a more or less secret knowledge or "recipe," a sense of the occasion or opportunity (*kairos*) of its use, a clearly delimited field of this use. (See Jean-Marie Pontévia, who takes up the analyses of Jean-Pierre Vernant in his *Tout a peut-être commencé par la beauté* [Bordeaux: William Blake & Co., 1985], pp. 42–44.) The "recipe" or the "trick" (the *Handgriff* of the "hidden art" of the Kantian schematism) goes along with the circumscription of the field, and together they define

an essential plurality of the *tekhnai*. "Art" would have ended up, at the moment of its supposed end, by retaining only the sense of the *kairos*, but joined to an infinite unfolding of the field (which becomes "presentation of the Idea") and of the "trick" (which becomes "genius"). It would have thus lost the plurality of the *tekhnai*. It would have erected itself as the improbable *tekhnē* of itself and of the absolute (of itself as absolute). On the becoming-art of the arts, one will find several very useful observations in Pierre-Damien Huyghe, "De la facture," Ph.D. diss., Strasbourg, 1994.

6. Heidegger, *The Origin of the Work of Art*, pp. 72–73.

7. Adorno, *Aesthetic Theory*, p. 15.

8. Immanuel Kant, *Critique of Judgment*, trans. J. H. Bernard (London: Hafner Press, 1951), §51, p. 164. Eliane Escoubas has analyzed very well the fragility of this partition, the way it reproduces the covering over of the whole by the part, and the extent to which it fails to contain all the arts under the definition of the model-art; see her *Imago mundi* (Paris: Galilée, 1986), pp. 68–79.

9. Kant, *Critique of Judgment*, §52.

10. F. W. J. Schelling, *The Philosophy of Art*, trans. Douglas W. Scott (Minneapolis: University of Minnesota Press, 1989), p. 45.

11. Ibid., p. 101.

12. *A*, 2: 613ff. On this whole genesis, one may also refer to Jean-Marie Schaeffer, *L'Art de l'âge moderne* (Paris: Gallimard, 1991), although the general orientation of his remarks is, to say the least, quite different.

13. See J.-L. Nancy, "Portrait de l'art en jeune fille," in *Le Poids d'une pensée* (Montréal: Le Griffon d'argile and Grenoble, Presses Universitaires de Grenoble, 1991); 2d version in *L'Art moderne et la question du sacré*, ed. Jean-Jacques Nillès (Paris: Cerf, 1993); the principle of the argument is also outlined in Nancy, *Le Sens du monde* (Paris: Galilée, 1993), pp. 199–200. We may add here that the whole schema of this analysis could be seen as having a strictly congruent version in the history of the work's producer: the succession of figures that can be designated the "artisan," the "genius," and the "artist."

14. *A*, 2: 621. Hegel is merely taking up a long tradition concerning the correspondence between the arts and the senses, amply attested since the neo-Platonism of the Italian Renaissance; see Luise Vinge, *The Five Senses* (Lund, Sweden: CWK Gleerup, 1975).

15. See, e.g., Erwin Straus in *The Primary World of Senses: A Vindication of Sensory Experience*, trans. Jacob Needleman (New York: Free Press of Glencoe, 1963).

16. "Synaesthetic perception is the rule," writes M. Merleau-Ponty (*Phenomenology of Perception*, trans. Colin Smith [New York: Humanities Press, 1962], p. 229). We disagree with G. Deleuze about the continuity that he seems to suppose between perceptive synesthesia (which he takes over from Merleau-Ponty) and the "existential communication" of the senses in artistic experience (see Deleuze, *Francis Bacon: Logique de la sensation* [Paris: Editions de La Différence, 1994], 1: 31. If there is indeed a unity or synthesis in the two cases, they are not of the same order, and this difference can be deciphered in Deleuze himself. We will come back to this. In Deleuze, one could also return to his proposed treatment of the difference between the *faculties* in the Kantian sense, each faculty being considered as the place of a singular exercise, irreducible to a "common sense."

17. Quoted by Vinge, *Five Senses*, p. 156.

18. In the French phrase *le singulier pluriel*, either word can be read as noun and adjective; moreover, like its English cognate, "singulier" means both "nonplural" and "odd, unusual, strange."—Trans.

19. Saint Augustine, *De quantitate animae*, XIV, 24, and Marsilio Ficino, *Teologia platonica*, 1, bk. vii. Cinema has as a recurring theme the kinesthesia of a penetration of the eye, as well as the presentation of a—more or less naive—"sublation" of all the arts: among many other examples, *Un Chien andalou* (Luis Buñuel, 1928), *2001: A Space Odyssey* (Stanley Kubrick, 1968), *Freejack* (Geoff Murphy, 1991).

20. In French, *du pâtir*: no common English verb easily renders the general sense of passivity, as in the reception of sense impressions.—Trans.

21. In French, *se sentir*: this reflexive construction is commonly used in expressions that report "personal" feelings: e.g., "je me sens malade," "je me sens triste"; "I feel sick," "I feel sad."—Trans.

22. See Pierre Rodrigo, "Comment dire la sensation? Logos et aisthesis en *De Anima*, III, 2," *Etudes phénoménologiques*, no. 16, 1992.

23. See Sigmund Freud, *Three Essays on the Theory of Sexuality*, trans. James Strachey (New York: Basic Books, 1962), p. 77.

24. Ibid., p. 99. Freud adds: "though there are some particularly marked erotogenic zones whose excitation would seem to be secured from the very first by certain organic contrivances."

25. Ibid., p. 76.

26. Perhaps one should say that every *aisthēsis* is pleasure, inasmuch as it is interested *aisthēsis*, first of all *interested in itself*, inasmuch as "feeling-

itself-feel" characterizes *aisthēsis* for Aristotle, rendering useless any sup-position of a "common sense." Pain, on the other hand, would be *aisthēsis* that repels itself, in the sense that it feels itself repel itself. See Nancy, *Le Sens du monde*, p. 226ff. See also the analyses proposed by Jérôme Porée in *La Philosophie à l'épreuve du mal: Pour une phénoménologie de la souffrance* (Paris: Vrin, 1994).

27. For all that, there has doubtless been too little thought given to what is implied by the disappearance of the "secondary" qualities in Descartes' piece of melted wax: their reciprocal exteriority is at once dissolved and *ex-posed there* in geometric extensivity.

28. Freud, *Three Essays*, p. 22.

29. *De rerum natura*, 11, 434–35. See also, among countless other examples, J. A. Brillat-Savarin: "Touch gave birth to all the arts, all the skills, all industry" (*La Physiologie du goût* [Paris: Hermann, 1975], p. 44), which does not prevent this author, following the example of several others, from adding to the five senses a *genesic* sense (or sense of "physical desire"), which cannot be reduced, according to him, to touch; mean-while, he does not invoke a sense of pain. It would require a long study to describe the variations of the *sensoria* according to different times and places.

30. "Le toucher n'est autre chose que la touche du sens tout entier": *le toucher* designates the sense of touch, while *la touche* is touch in the sense of a touch of genius or the quality of a painter's brush stroke.—Trans.

31. Jacques Derrida, "*Le toucher*: Touch/To Touch Him," trans. Peggy Kamuf, *Paragraph* 16, no. 2 (1993): 127.

32. In Merleau-Ponty's terms, as these are taken up and prolonged by Marc Richir in "Phénoménologie des couleurs": "Colors are not first of all the colors of things, but colors *of world* . . . there are no phenomena-of-world except in the plural and in an indefinite referring back from one to the other" (in *La Couleur* [Brussels: Editions Ousia, 1993], p. 186). We may add: "One image must be transformed through contact with other images, just as a color is transformed in contact with other colors. A blue is not the same blue when it is next to a green, a yellow, a red. No art without transformation." This fragment is immediately followed by another: "The cinematographer's 'true' cannot be the theater's, nor the novel's, nor painting's." (Robert Bresson, *Notes sur le cinématographe* [Paris: Gallimard, 1975], p. 16.)

33. For two excellent formulations of the thing in itself, see first, concerning Kant, Corinne Énaudeau: "There are not, however, two

things, the one latent, real, the other manifest, illusory, but just one: the existing phenomenon. The thing in itself is not a cause of the phenomenon, exterior to it (it has as a cause only other phenomena); it is not a background, substance, substratum that finds in the phenomenon a path of disfigured expression. It is strictly the same "thing" as the phenomenon, but insofar as it would not appear" ("Le psychique en soi," *Nouvelle Revue de Psychanalyse* 48 (Autumn 1993): 43). Second, see Werner Hamacher: "Hegel's formulation that space is *die Äusserlichkeit an ihm selbst* [exteriority right at itself] corrects the massive and wholly unfounded privilege given to the exterior by way of its seemingly inconspicuous *an*: space is—and thus *is* not—not exteriority, but atteriority, laterality. . . . The Thing *an* itself (*Ding* an *sich*). Space. Parataxis" ("Amphora [Extracts]" trans. Dana Hollander, *Assemblage* 20, "Violence Space," ed. Mark Wigley [April 1993], p. 40).

34. Heidegger, "Die Kunst und der Raum" (St. Gallen: Erker Verlag, 1969), p. 11. It is no coincidence, of course, that this text sketches an analysis of space and of spacing (i.e., of the motif acknowledged to be irreducible by the analyses of *Being and Time*; see Heidegger, *On Time and Being*, trans. Joan Stambaugh [New York: Harper and Row, 1972], p. 23) with regard to art, and to art insofar as it is implicitly acknowledged to be irreducible to the subsumption under *Dichtung* asserted in *The Origin of the Work of Art*. An attentive examination would show that Heidegger began there, as if in spite of himself, a conjoint analysis of "local" spacing and of the difference between the arts.

35. That is why it is remarkable that the metaphysics (and no doubt the theology) of creation oscillates between complete reduction (the God of Spinoza is the world, not its creator, even if Spinoza keeps the term; see the refutation of the *ex nihilo*, *Cogitata Metaphysica*, x) and identification with a technical operation and/or artist, of which the best example, already prepared for by Descartes, is the God of Leibniz: choosing between all possible worlds, which he sees, He is already "in the world" of all these possibles.

36. L. Wittgenstein, *Remarks on Colour*, trans. Linda L. McAlister and Margarete Schättle (Berkeley: University of California Press, 1978), pp. 50e–51e.

37. *A*, 1: 153–54.

38. Paul Valéry, *Cahiers*, vol. 2 (Paris: Gallimard, 1987), p. 945. See also pp. 967–68: "How is hearing questions and answers by itself alone? There is 'ornament' when there is proper organization of the sensorial

values in some domain of the senses that contains stimulants and re-
spondents—whereas ordinary perceptions have responses that are either
null or meaningful and are, from the *accidental* to the *meaningful,*
passages and expedients." That one art consists in "depriving itself" of
the others, and that this mutual "deprivation" brings about their "circular
ring" or their "musaic hyperbaton" is proposed by Michel Deguy in *La
Poésie n'est pas seule* (Paris: Editions du Seuil, 1990).

39. Plato, *Theia moira, Ion,* 534c and other passages. On this motif, see
J.-L. Nancy, "Sharing Voices," in Gayle L. Ormiston and Alan D.
Schrift, eds., *Transforming the Hermeneutic Context: From Nietzsche to
Nancy* (Albany: State University of New York Press, 1990), pp. 229–34. In
the *Ion,* the poet, in the figure of the rhapsode, is accused of lacking
tekhnē, at least to the extent that he claims, under the influence of the
Muse, to speak something of the divine. But it is also a way of designating
a *tekhnē* that cannot be found in the manner of the *tekhnai* that have
well-defined works proper to them and to which all the "arts" belong.
Thus the alternative is: either recognize a supplementary *tekhnē,* a *tekhnē*
of the "divine lot" and of its "touch," or submit all the *tekhnai* to the
jurisdiction of the philosophical *epistēmē,* which knows all about the
divine *demiurgy* of the world.

40. "Smells, colors, and sounds respond to each other"—but one must
not misunderstand this. Baudelaire is perfectly aware of the *discreteness* of
the arts (which Nietzsche, during the same period, deplores): "Is it
through a fatefulness of several kinds of decadence that today each art
manifests the urge to trespass on the neighboring art, and that painters
introduce musical scales into painting, sculptors color into sculpture,
writers plastic means into literature?" (*Ecrits esthétiques* [Paris: Christian
Bourgois, 1986], p. 268).

41. Deleuze, *Francis Bacon,* p. 31.

42. In this regard, one may recall E. Benveniste's analysis of the word
"rhythm" as designating "form in the instant that it is assumed by what is
moving, mobile, and fluid, the form of that which does not have organic
consistency" (*Problems of General Linguistics,* trans. Mary Elizabeth Meek
[Coral Gables, Fla.: University of Miami Press, 1971], pp. 285–86). One
should add to this that Plato's *khōra* is very close to *ruthmos,* perhaps
more like its flip side (the fluid that assumes form), even though Plato
does not use the two words in the same context. (But Benveniste notes
that Plato already applied a metric constraint to *ruthmos,* one which is
unknown to *khōra*; in this regard, rhythm could also be "arhythmic.")

Now *khōra*, the opening of the general or generic "place," the place or the "abyssal chasm" (Jacques Derrida, "Khōra," trans. Ian McLeod, in *On the Name*, ed. Thomas Dutoit [Stanford: Stanford University Press, 1995], p. 104) of plasticity and the originary *mimēsis* out of which the world comes, is precisely, as such, that from which there can be the diversity of elements as such. From *khōra* to *aisthēsis* and no doubt to *tekhnai*, there is a continuity of heterogeneous provenance and even, more properly, *heterogenesis*. But *khōra* "itself" is nothing but the stuff of difference, or the elasticity of spacing. For an "aesthetic of rhythms," see the essay by Henri Maldiney that is so titled, to which Deleuze refers, in *Regard Parole Espace* (Lausanne: L'Age d'Homme, 1973). As for *ruthmos*, one would have to take up again, in its relation with *phusis*, the analysis that Heidegger outlines in "On the Being and Conception of *Physis* in Aristotle's *Physics*," trans. Thomas Sheehan, *Man and World* 4 (1977).

43. See Marc Groenen, "Colorants et symbolique au paléolithique," in *La Couleur*.

44. Thierry de Duve, *Au nom de l'art* (Paris: Editions de Minuit, 1989), p. 138.

45. What we are saying here too quickly supposes a close explication of the Heideggerian motifs of *phusis* and "technics." These motifs are as famous as they are misinterpreted. Far too briefly: Heidegger does not understand *phusis* as "production of/by itself," but quite differently as "coming into presence" or "coming into being." And "technics" is today the mode in which this "coming" unfolds. It is thus far from constituting the object of the simple critical debasement imputed to Heidegger, (which, it should be said, he himself has largely induced). In order to see this, one must carefully reread texts such as "On the Being and Conception of *Physis* in Aristotle's *Physics*" and *The Principle of Reason*. We will do so.

46. The terms translated by "ground" and "grounds" are *fond*, *fonds*. The latter form also has the sense of fund or funds.—Trans.

47. Alain Badiou, *Conditions* (Paris: Editions du Seuil, 1992), p. 361. A little further on, Badiou writes of "the Infinite of the sensible" (p. 363). See also Valéry: "real things act aesthetically through this [sensible] multiplicity that prevents one from having done with them through an abstract act" (*Cahiers*, 2: 942).

48. *A*, 2: 968.

49. See, e.g., *A*, 2: 1013: "even if in poetry [the sound of words] merely

chimes in as an external medium, it still must be treated as an end in itself, and shaped therefore within harmonious limits." Hegel goes so far as to characterize the passage from Greek poetry to modern poetry as the passage from a less "internal" poetry and a more immediately sensuous prosody to a more "inward and spiritual" poetry that, "in order to reestablish the rights of the sensuous element," requires recourse to rhyme as to a "material medium of sound," which is "most correspondent" to this poetry that "strikes more strongly the soul-laden note of feeling" (p. 1023). On art as "languages," let us cite Henri Maldiney: "Art is not made of signs but of forms, and if we call it a language, we must recast the meaning of speech. The difference between sign and form is summed up in this remark by Henri Focillon: 'The sign signifies, whereas the form signifies *itself*' [*Vie des formes* (Paris: Presses Universitaires de France, 1981), p. 4]. The sign is not of the same order as what it signifies. Things are altogether different with artistic, and therefore aesthetic, form. Its signification is one with its appearing" ("Esthétique des rythmes," p. 131).

50. *A*, 2: 977. Hegel employs *Partikularität* to designate the particular determination in its exteriority and in the closure of its immediacy, rather than in its mediated derivation from generic unity.

51. *Tekhnē* exhibits the end, puts it at a distance, and makes visible the operation of the "in view of," that is, of sense perceptibly divided from its effectuation. It is thus that it serves as a model for thinking a finality of *phusis*: see Aristotle, *Physics*, 199 a–b.

52. Derrida, *Khōra*, p. 111.

53. This question gets multiplied right away: what aspect for which eye, what smell for which nose, what sound for which ear, what consistency for which touch, what movement for which kinoreceptor, and so forth. The philosophical and poetic tradition will have exhausted all these possibilities.

54. *A*, 2: 976.

55. Paul Celan, "The Meridian," trans. Rosmarie Waldrop, in *Paul Celan: Collected Prose* (Riverdale-on-Hudson, N.Y.: The Sheep Meadow Press, 1986), p. 50. See Philippe Lacoue-Labarthe, *La Poésie comme expérience* (Paris: Christian Bourgois, 1986), p. 98. Lacoue-Labarthe himself operates a chiasmus of the two senses of sense when further on he writes: "In the thing or the singular being that it is incumbent upon poetry—upon the poem—to perceive (to think)."

56. Alberto Caeiro/Fernando Pessoa, *The Keeper of Sheep*, trans. Edwin Honig and Susan M. Brown (Riverdale-on-Hudson, N.Y.: The Sheep Meadow Press, 1986), p. 52.

57. This phrase, *être-au-monde*, is generally translated "being-in-the-world."—Trans.

58. Hubert Damisch, *Ruptures, Cultures* (Paris: Editions de Minuit, 1976), p. 189.

59. Gérard Lépinlois, "La vallée de la figuration," unpublished text on Pirandello's *I Giganti della montagna*.

60. Edmund Husserl, *Ideas: General Introduction to Pure Phenomenology*, trans. W. R. Boyce Gibson (New York: Macmillan, 1931), p. 169.

61. The two phrases in question are highly idiomatic in French. On the one hand, in the idiomatic expression "il y a de l'évidence," the pronoun *il* is impersonal and indefinite. The common English translation by "there is" loses the point. On the other hand, "il, c'est lui qui est évident" depends on a repetition of the subject in the tonic pronoun *lui*, which has no grammatically marked equivalent in English.—Trans.

62. Adorno, *Aesthetic Theory*, p. 258.

63. Freud comes close to recognizing this when he places the origin of "individual psychology" in the first poetic-mythic invention (in *Group Psychology and Analysis of the Ego*, Appendix B; see also *Totem and Taboo* and Sarah Kofman, *The Childhood of Art: An Interpretation of Freud's Aesthetics*, trans. Winifred Woodhull (New York: Columbia University Press, 1988), p. 15. Generally, it is in the end a matter of initiating a deconstruction of religion, first of all the religion or religions of "creation." Instead of falling back into "the problematic of the recreation of the world: in a space that is once again illusionist" (Jean-Claude Lebensztejn, *Zigzag* [Paris: Aubier-Flammarion, 1981], p. 74), it is a matter of deconstructing creation. We will come back to this elsewhere. The question of the arts would not merit attention (artists having taken it well in hand) if it did not hide the stakes of a beyond-religion which is now ineluctable—but of a beyond that owes nothing to the (bourgeois, as no one dares to say anymore) cult of Art.

64. See at least this sentence of Bernard Stiegler: "If technics can be an end in itself, that means that the opposition of ends and means no longer thinks far enough" (*La Technique et le temps 1* [Paris: Galilée, 1994], p. 107. Stiegler also writes: "We fully grasp the sense of *tekhnē* only in art, which is its highest form." Despite the convergence, we would most likely not

subscribe to this last formulation, to the extent that it risks causing a misunderstanding about the moment of the "vanishing" or "nonappearance" of art. At the moment of writing, I do not yet have sufficient familiarity with Stiegler's important work. In a convergent manner, Sylviane Agacinski seeks, in a reflection on the museum and the exhibition, to overcome an opposition between the "respectful" aesthetic gaze and the technical gaze animated by "the cruelty of seeing and knowing" (*Volume* [Paris: Galilée, 1992], pp. 179–80). Agacinski gives this indication, as well: "Rather than saying that there exist technical or mechanized periods of 'art,' one might say—while remaining very close to what is most novel in Benjamin—that all the *arts* inscribe themselves, always, and sometimes invent themselves, in a period of technics" ("Le Passager: Modernité du photographique," in *Rue Descartes*, no. 10, 1994, p. 31).

65. Wassily Kandinsky, *Concerning the Spiritual in Art* (New York: George Wittenborn, Inc., 1947), pp. 84–85. Translation modified.

Chapter 2

1. Here we resume and extend the analysis proposed in "Portrait de l'art en jeune fille," first published in *Le Poids d'une pensée* (Montreal: Le Griffon d'argile, and Grenoble: Presses Universitaires de Grenoble, 1992), then, somewhat modified, in Jean-Jacques Nillès, ed., *L'Art moderne et la question du sacré* (Paris: Cerf, 1993), as well as the complementary material to be found in *Nium*, co-authored with François Martin (Valence: Editions Erba, 1993), p. 48ff.

2. We note, without being able to comment further here, that in Hegel one will seek in vain this paradoxical inverse "sublation" of the speculative by the poetic, unless one takes as exemplary evidence the fact that *The Phenomenology of Spirit* ends with lines by Schiller. This *coda* of the *Phenomenology* conforms to the requirement of the "speculative proposition" as it is presented in the Preface: "This conflict between the general form of a proposition and the unity of the Notion which destroys it is similar to the conflict that occurs in rhythm between metre and accent. Rhythm results from the floating centre and the unification of the two. So, too, in the philosophical proposition the identification of Subject and Predicate . . . is meant to emerge as a harmony." This poetics of philosophical prose becomes, a little later, a plastics: "only a philosophical exposition that rigidly excludes the usual way of relating the parts of a

proposition could achieve the goal of plasticity" (*PS*, 38–39). "Plastics" is the word for the pure (trans)formation of interiority into exteriority, or for the pure (con)formation of the latter to the former; it is thereby the word for the pure extra-position of interiority, which no longer retains any interior. One might wonder whether the "speculative poetry" which may thereby be required should not be sought, in a more subtle or devious manner yet in keeping with a very Hegelian logic, in the political order, but it would then be in a form yet to be (re)born, as this passage from the *Aesthetics* might indicate: "For the whole state of the world today has assumed a form diametrically opposed in its prosaic organization to the requirements which we found irremissible for genuine epic, and the revolutions to which the recent circumstances of states and peoples have been subject *are still too fixed in our memory as actual experiences to be compatible with the epic form of art*" (*A*, 2: 1109; emphasis added).

3. Hegel describes the specificity proper to painting thus: "The free subjectivity allows independent existence to the entire range of things in nature and all spheres of human activity, yet it can enter into every particular thing and make it into material for inner contemplation; indeed, only in this involvement with concrete reality does it prove itself to be concrete and living" (*A*, 2: 803; trans. modified).

4. The translation has been corrected in accordance with the indications given by J.-F. Lefebvre in his French translation (*Phénoménologie de l'esprit* [Paris: Aubier, 1991], pp. 489–90), as noted in our prior publication in *L'Art moderne et la question du sacré*. One should recall that the Pantheon, that properly Roman place of religion (which is, as we shall see, the temple of a tendency toward the dissolution of religion) has for Hegel two faces: on the one hand, it is, as here, the place of the preserved unity of the vanished Greek gods; on the other hand, it will be, in the *Aesthetics*, "the wide Pantheon of art" as the "external actualization" of the "particular arts" and "individual works of art" (*A*, 1: 90). The unity of this double Pantheon is precisely plurality and exteriority; that of the Greek gods is, on the one hand, that of the "particular arts," on the other, and *between* the two, exteriority *as such* (about which one will always have to say that it cannot be *as such* from the moment it is no longer to be related to an interiority that precedes or follows it).

5. Thus Hegel can represent in a particularly ambivalent or not clearly decidable manner the maintenance of religion alongside philosophy: "Religion must be for all men, for those who have purified their thinking

in such a way that they have knowledge of what is in the pure element of thought, for those who have achieved a speculative knowledge of what God is, as well as for those who have not risen above feeling and representation. Man is not solely a pure activity of thinking, but thought itself is made manifest as intuition and as representation; absolute truth, which has been revealed to man, must also be for him inasmuch as he is endowed with representation, with intuition, and for him inasmuch as he is endowed with feeling, with sensation." (Hegel, "Proofs of the Existence of God," in Hegel, *Lectures on the Philosophy of Religion*, trans. E. B. Spiers (New York: Humanities Press, 1974), 3: 309.) It then becomes difficult to discern what would distinguish religion from art, all the more so in that certain aspects of this text strike a more "Catholic" note (at least as concerns "sensation") than a "Protestant" one.

6. Hegel, *Lectures on the History of Philosophy*, trans. E. S. Haldane and Frances H. Simson (New York: Humanities Press, 1974), 1: 276. This text is from 1829–30. One hardly need exercise interpretive violence to think that this "secret" of art, if it is secret because art keeps its true finality veiled beneath pure form whereas philosophy declares this finality, is also a secret for Hegel, who only guesses it or confesses it slowly and with difficulty—unless he does not dare to declare it because of his public position.

7. In the Lectures of 1827, Hegel notes, with reference to the construction of the Egyptian pyramids and other architectural monuments, "The colossal diligence of an entire people was not yet in and for itself pure fine art; rather it was the impulsion toward fine art" (*PR*, 634).

8. This is indicated by a passage from the *Aesthetics* (2: 800). At this chapter's opening, we have reproduced one of several engravings of a girl bearing offerings, from the book, which Hegel certainly knew, that Christophe, Count von Muhr, began to publish in 1777: *Abbildungen der Gemälde und Alterthümer welche seit 1738 sowohl in der verschütteten Stadt Herkulanum als auch in den umliegenden Gegenden an das Licht gebracht worden* . . . (Augsburg: Christian Deckhardt). The engraving comes from vol. 2, published in 1778. Doubtless, it will always be possible to think that Hegel could have made his allusion clearer. But one could think the same of other references in the *Phenomenology*. Moreover, here there are traces of the "secret" we have already discussed, to which we might join the hypothesis of another secret: the girl Nanette Endel, a platonic love of his youth, who sent Hegel a present of flowers, which were dried out when they arrived but kept about them "the spiritual life"

(Hegel, letter dated July 2, 1797, with postscript dated July 17). Hegel was perhaps remembering these flowers when he said, about Italian painters, that "in beauty itself their concern is not with beauty of form alone, not with that sensuous unity of the soul with its body which is effused over the sensuous corporeal forms, but instead with this trait of love and reconciliation in each figure, form, and individuality of character. It is the butterfly, the Psyche, which in the sunlight of its heaven hovers even over withered flowers" (*A*, 2: 875).

9. The offering of fruits is perhaps also, and according to several ancient traditions (which are extended in more than one modern painting), the offering of the breasts. Several of the bearers of offerings from Pompeii have bare breasts. The one we have reproduced was chosen, by contrast, for the direction of her gaze. One could present a lengthy commentary on the *discrete* and *discreet* transition from the girl to the Virgin Mary as principal subject of "romantic painting," to her grace mixed with grandeur, to the maternal and nourishing offering of her breasts.

10. See also this passage: "In supreme art we see fixed the most fleeting appearance of the sky, the time of day, the lighting of the trees; the appearances and reflections of clouds, waves, lochs, streams; the shimmering and glittering of wine in a glass, a flash of the eye, a momentary look or smile, etc. . . . painting may not spurn this subject-matter which on its side and alone is fitted to be treated with such art and to provide this infinite subtlety and delicacy of pure appearance" (*A*, 2: 812–13).

11. "Why, at the moment when through the force of the times art disappears, does it appear for the first time as a search in which something essential is at stake, where what counts is no longer the artist or active labor or any of the values upon which the world is built or even any of the other values upon which formerly the beyond opened? And why is this search nonetheless precise, rigorous, bent upon culminating in a work, in a work which *is*, and nothing more?" (Maurice Blanchot, *The Space of Literature*, trans. Ann Smock (Lincoln: University of Nebraska Press, 1982), p. 220.

Chapter 3

N O T E : This text was read at the Louvre in front of *The Death of the Virgin*, by Caravaggio, on June 22, 1992; the French text was first published in *Po&sie* 64 (1993); the English translation is reprinted, with permission, from *Paragraph* 16, 2 (July 1993).

Chapter 4

N O T E : The first version of this essay was published in an issue of *La Part de l'oeil* (no. 10, 1994) devoted to Georges Bataille and aesthetics. Besides differences in the text, the original publication was that of the handwritten manuscript, traversing original designs by the painter François Martin. A facsimile of one of these pages is reproduced here.

Chapter 5

N O T E : This text was originally delivered at the Jeu de Paume and was subsequently published in *L'Art contemporain en question* (Paris: Jeu de Paume, 1994).

1. Jean-Louis Déotte, *Le Musée, origine de l'esthétique* (Paris: L'Harmattan, 1993).

2. Quoted in ibid., p. 17.

3. Theodor W. Adorno, *Negative Dialectics*, trans. E. B. Ashton (New York: The Seabury Press, 1973), p. 367.

4. Michel Leiris, *Journal 1922–1989* (Paris: Gallimard, 1992), p. 154.

5. Immanuel Kant, *Critique of Judgment*, §47.

6. Ernest Renan, *Dialogues et fragments philosophiques* (n.p., n.d.), Second Dialogue, "Probabilités," p. 83. M. Duchamp, quoted in Nella Arambasin, *La Conception du sacré dans la critique d'art en Europe entre 1880 et 1914*, Ph.D. diss., University of Paris-Sorbonne, 1992, 1: 204. This thesis contains a mine of valuable information concerning the consideration of the "end of art" and its effects within art and within the discours on art during the period studied.

7. Jan Patocka has introduced reflections in this direction; see *L'Art et le temps*, French trans. E. Abrams (Paris: POL, 1990).

8. In French: "tout l'art tel qu'en lui-même enfin," which echos the first line of Mallarmé's "Tombeau pour Edgar Poe."—Trans.

9. Joseph Conrad, Preface to *The Nigger of the "Narcissus"* (Oxford: Oxford University Press, 1984), p. xxxix.

10. Norman Mailer, *Pieces and Pontifications* (Boston: Little, Brown, 1982), p. 46.

11. Jean Dubuffet, *Prospectus et tous écrits suivants*, vol. 1 (Paris: Gallimard, 1967), p. 79.

12. M. Merleau-Ponty, *Eye and Mind*, trans. Carleton Dallery, in *The Essential Writings of Merleau-Ponty*, ed. Alden L. Fisher (New York: Harcourt, Brace & World, 1969), p. 284.

13. Plotinus, *Enneads*, 2.6.

14. Friedrich Nietzsche, *Werke in drei Bänden*, ed. Karl Schlechta, vol. 3 (Munich: Carl Hanser Verlag, 1958), p. 617.

15. Adorno, *Negative Dialectics*, p. 402.

16. Thomas Aquinas, *Summa Theologiae*, 1a, q. 45, art. 7. On the image and vestige, in Thomas Aquinas and elsewhere, one should consult the analyses of Georges Didi-Huberman in his *Fra Angelico: Dissemblance et figuration* (Paris: Flammarion, 1990). I diverge from him by proposing a nondialectical interpretation of the *vestigium*; however, in the context of theology, Didi-Huberman's dialectical interpretation is absolutely correct.

17. One can further compare it, among other examples, with Rembrandt's *The Anatomy Lesson of Doctor Joan Deyman*.

18. With the association of *plante (du pied)* and of *plat*, the text signals toward some idiomatic expressions in French: for example, *mettre les pieds dans le plat* (to put one's foot down, but also to put one's foot in it) or a *pieds-plats* (an awkward individual, a lout).—Trans.

19. To evoke the *pas* is to salute Blanchot and Derrida.

20. On the question of the figure, see Philippe Lacoue-Labarthe and Jean-Luc Nancy, "Scène," in *Nouvelle Revue de Psychanalyse*, Fall 1992.

21. Dante, *Inferno*, VIII, 27, and XII, 29.

22. This time the salute goes to Thierry de Duve ("Do anything whatsoever . . . "), *Au nom de l'art* (Paris: Editions de Minuit, 1981).

23. The common French term *gens* has no simple equivalent in English. When used in a general or indefinite sense, it is ordinarily translated as "people."—Trans.

MERIDIAN

Crossing Aesthetics

Library of Congress
Cataloging-in-Publication Data

Nancy, Jean-Luc.
[Les muses. English]
The muses / Jean-Luc Nancy ; translated by Peggy Kamuf.
p.   cm. — (Meridian, crossing aesthetics)
Includes bibliographical references (p.   ).
ISBN 0-8047-2780-5 (cloth : alk. paper). — ISBN 0-8047-2781-3
(pbk. : alk. paper)
1. Aesthetics.   2. Arts.   3. Art—Philosophy.   I. Title.
II. Series: Meridian (Stanford, Calif.)
BH39.N2713   1996
701—dc20   96-10880   CIP

⊗ This book is printed on acid-free, recycled paper.
It was typeset in Adobe Garamond and Lithos
by Keystone Typesetting, Inc.

Original printing 1996

Last figure below indicates year of this printing:

05   04   03   02   01   00   99   98   97   96